P9-CFJ-180

DISCARD

BEETHOVEN'S HAIR

BEETHOVEN'S HAIR

RUSSELL MARTIN

BROADWAY BOOKS   NEW YORK

BROADWAY

Broadway Books titles may be purchased for business or promotional use or for special sales. For information, please write to: Special Markets Department, Random House, Inc., 1540 Broadway, New York, NY 10036.

BROADWAY BOOKS and its logo, a letter B bisected on the diagonal, are trademarks of Broadway Books, a division of Random House, Inc.

Visit our website at www.broadwaybooks.com

Library of Congress Cataloging-in-Publication Data
Martin, Russell.
Beethoven's hair / Russell Martin.—1st ed.
p.   cm.
1. Beethoven, Ludwig van, 1770–1827—Relics.
2. Beethoven, Ludwig van, 1770–1827—Death and burial.
3. Hiller, Ferdinand, 1811–1885. I. Title.
ML410.B4.M28 2000
780'.92—dc21   00-031233

FIRST EDITION
Designed by Bonni Leon-Berman

ISBN 0-7679-0350-1
00 01 02 03 04 10 9 8 7 6 5 4 3 2

KH

Alive again? then show me where he is:
I'll give a thousand pound to look upon him.
He hath no eyes, the dust hath blinded them.
Comb down his hair: look! look! it stands upright,
Like lime-twigs set to catch my winged soul.

WILLIAM SHAKESPEARE,
HENRY THE SIXTH, PART 2

Oh, it would be so lovely to live a thousand lives.

LUDWIG VAN BEETHOVEN,
IN A LETTER TO FRANZ
WEGELER

CONTENTS

PRELUDE

Beethoven's hair, sheltered for nearly two centuries inside a glass locket, was about to become the subject of rapt attention on a warm December morning in 1995. The two men principally involved in its purchase—Brooklyn-born Ira Brilliant, a retired Phoenix real estate developer, and a Mexican-American physician whose surprising name is Che Guevara—had been joined by a coterie of inquisitors in a teaching theater at the University of Arizona Medical Center in Tucson: a forensic anthropologist was present; so were a medical examiner, an archivist and conservator, a medical photographer, a recording secretary, a notary public, a local television news team, plus a London-based film crew from the BBC. Everyone gathered promptly at 10:30 because there was much to do, and the first order of business was the signing of a contract that stipulated how the hair would be divided. Once counted, strand by aging and fragile strand, 27 percent would remain the property of Dr. Alfredo "Che" Guevara, the principal investor, a urological surgeon from the border town of Nogales. The remainder would be donated by him and Brilliant to the Ira F. Brilliant Center for Beethoven Studies at San Jose State University in California, where it would remain in perpetuity.

Contract signed and the notary's seal correctly affixed, soon it was time to turn to the locket that held the hair. Housed in a dark-wood oval frame a bit more than ten centimeters long, the coil of fine brown and gray hair was sealed between two pieces of glass, one of which was convex. On the brittle paper that was sealed to the flat back of the frame, someone named Paul Hiller long ago had written the following words in German, then added his signature beneath them:

This hair was cut off Beethoven's corpse by my father, Dr. Ferdinand v. Hiller on the day after Ludwig van Beethoven's death, that is, on 27 March 1827, and was given to me as a birthday present in Cologne on May 1, 1883.

While Ira Brilliant and the others watched with fascination, Dr. Guevara and conservator Nancy Odegaard—both dressed

in green surgical scrubs and wearing masks and gloves—
worked at a sterile table, measuring with calipers the glass and
the frame that surrounded it, calling out a series of numbers as
well as their impressions of the locket's condition before
Guevara wielded a scalpel and prepared to go inside. This *was*
surgery of a sort, and the doctor proceeded with careful confidence, describing each cut and every observation with the
kind of commentary he might have made if the subject at hand
had been a human gut and the gathered observers were surgical interns still prone to getting queasy. "Now I'm slicing
through the last of the glue that holds the paper backing," he
announced, his voice bearing more than a hint of his preoccu-
pation. "I'll pull the backing away now, and . . . let's see,
below . . . here's another layer of paper, with writing on it,
and . . . the writing's in French, I believe. Can someone verify
that this is in French and translate it for us?"

A video camera designed for recording the intricacies and
complexities of rather more conventional surgeries looked
down from overhead and the rest of the group watched the
doctor's work on television monitors placed around the room,
and yes, that *was* French, someone offered. The text was set in
type, but was difficult to make sense of, and the room's quick
consensus was that the paper was simply newspaper scrap that
had been used for backing. Yet the words written on the next
layer Guevara exposed were both decipherable and surprising.
Handwritten this time, and again in German, they explained
that the locket was "newly pasted" by a picture framer in
Cologne in 1911, the resealing done at a time when Paul
Hiller would have been fifty-eight years old, and presumably

about the time when he wrote his explanatory note on the outer paper.

At last the surgeon held nothing more than the conjoined pieces of glass in his gloved hands, and Odegaard helped steady the glass on edge as Guevara began to break the seal with a scalpel. "Wow, could you hear that?" he asked. "I heard a rush of air like a vacuum when I started to separate the glass." Two minutes passed as the surgeon's knife slowly circumnavigated the oval, then finally the pieces were free and Guevara delicately lifted the domed glass away from its mate, and although no one spoke for a moment, you could sense the massed excitement. Exposed for the first time in at least eight decades, perhaps many more, *there* was Beethoven's hair—darker than it appeared under glass, a carefully shaped coil containing a hundred or two hundred strands, one of the group guessed. When he had been helped with the straps that held his mask over his nose, Guevara bent to the table to smell the hair. It was odorless, he declared, then Ira Brilliant and the others pressed forward to get close to the remarkable relic themselves.

Before the morning ended and the team adjourned for something of a celebratory lunch, Beethoven's hair was photographed, weighed, and examined under a high-power microscope. Forensic anthropologist Walter Birkby declared that on quick inspection the condition of the hair appeared consistent with hair that was approximately two hundred years old; he noted that it appeared to be free of lice—or the carcasses of lice—and the group was delighted when he noted as well that follicles were attached to at least some of the strands. Fifteen-year-old Ferdinand Hiller must have pulled at the hair as he snipped it—that was the initial supposition—and the fact that the boy inadvertently pulled a few follicles from Beethoven's scalp meant DNA testing might indeed be feasible, a possibility that none of the group had dared count on till that moment.

The cameras continued to roll at a press conference in the early afternoon, and the team outlined publicly for the first time the array of tests it planned to undertake. Prior to examining the hair's DNA—if that were done—likely there would be examinations to determine whether opiates had been in Beethoven's system at the time of his death. Other analyses would search for trace metals in his hair: high levels of zinc might mean that his immune system had been severely compromised; the presence of mercury could indicate that he had been treated for an infection, and elevated levels of mercury might even go some distance toward explaining Beethoven's notoriously eccentric behavior; an abundance of lead would point to one potential cause of the composer's deafness, and even might explain the concert of other maladies that had plagued him throughout his adult life.

Drawing on techniques and testing procedures that were established when a lock of Napoleon's hair was studied in the 1970s—tests that concluded that the emperor had *not* been poisoned, contrary to what many historians long had suspected—the Beethoven tests would be designed to destroy or permanently alter only a very minimal amount of the hair he had just unlocked, Guevara informed the assembled reporters.

And the tests would be carried out only by highly qualified scientists: "We're going to prepare a protocol to do the work under strict conditions that are forensic, sterile, and modern. We plan to tabulate people who have FBI-quality expertise, then invite them to propose specific tests to us. But we won't sacrifice the bulk of the hair. The main thing is our hope that two hundred years from now people won't think that there were neophytes at work who couldn't get their act together. Twenty-five or fifty years ago, this kind of testing wouldn't have been possible. And fifty years from now, maybe we'll get much more information."

But the newspaper and television reporters wanted to know more: they needed some sense of what motivated Guevara and his partner to buy the hair and now begin the process of having it rigorously examined. What was it about Beethoven that so obsessed them?

"My interest in Beethoven is like a fire burning inside me," answered seventy-three-year-old Ira Brilliant, his Brooklyn accent diluted only a bit by thirty years of expatriation in Arizona. "I started collecting his letters and first editions twenty years ago out of a deep wish to own something Beethoven himself had touched. It was my way of paying homage to his greatness." A short man whose dense eyebrows and deep-set eyes seemed to mirror the composer's, Ira Brilliant explained that on a November day almost a year earlier, he phoned Guevara, his friend and fellow Beethoven zealot, soon after he had seen the lock of hair listed in a Sotheby's catalog, and the two had agreed that they would try to make it theirs. "This was much more than simply something Beethoven had touched. The hair *is* Beethoven. It's a marvelous relic."

And the doctor agreed, of course. A large man with a thick shock of black hair atop his head, his speech inflected with echoes of his native Spanish—and "Che" to his friends since his long-ago college days—Guevara's obsession with both Beethoven's music and Beethoven the man tumbled out of him with a kind of evangelical passion. "Beethoven was deaf, as you know. He suffered from kidney stones, which is a very painful condition. He had hepatitis; he had multiple episodes of gastrointestinal infections. For someone to have that many maladies and to suffer so greatly and yet produce superhuman music, music that can actually elevate the spirit to a much different plane than the ordinary plane we live in, is quite phenomenal."

Beethoven's hair—still in the same coil in which it was wrapped nearly two centuries ago, the hundreds of separate strands still waiting to be counted—had been removed for safekeeping, but Che Guevara spoke of it as though it remained in the room: "To get this close to a man who was able to do this . . . for me it's a personal triumph. Acquiring the hair already has changed my life."

ON A WARM MAY AFTERNOON a hundred and seventy years before, Beethoven's hair would have spread wildly out from his head and the dark eyes beneath it would have appeared small but piercingly bright as he made his daily walk through the city. His complexion was swarthy, his forehead broad and high, and much of his face had been pockmarked by smallpox back when he was a boy. He was short, even by the standards of his day, and because of intestinal troubles that by 1824 had plagued him for three decades, no longer was he the stout and stocky man he once had been. He would have walked with a lumbering gait that spring, one that evidenced a curious kind of clumsiness, and he would not have heard the din of the grand and boisterous city in which he trod—not the constant racket of vendors' carts and carriages, nor the cacophonous noise of the jugglers, puppeteers, and street musicians who seemed to clog every corner; neither the kindly proffered greetings of acquaintances nor the taunts of the urchins who tagged at his heels. The deafness that twenty years before had begun to rob him of the subtlest kinds of sounds inexorably had reduced his world to animated and very isolated silence, and by now he could hear only what his mind imagined.

Yet Ludwig van Beethoven, this strange and eccentric figure—who once had been arrested as a vagrant—was at that moment, in fact, the most celebrated composer in a city filled to its exquisite rooftops with composers. His Ninth Symphony had been premiered only days before to the most glorious kind of acclaim. He had become a true legend in Vienna in the three decades since he had made the city his home, and his bold, passionate, and altogether revolutionary compositions already seemed destined to endure. The people who would have greeted or simply recognized him as walked that afternoon would have understood that Herr Beethoven was aging quickly and clearly was not well. But at least his music, they would have warranted, would survive for centuries.

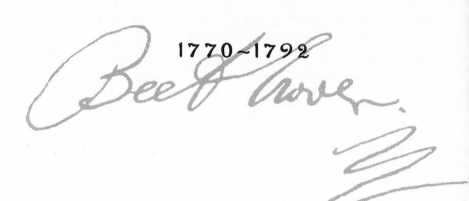

1770–1792

LUDWIG VAN BEETHOVEN HAD BEEN his grandfather's name as well, and although he was not quite three when his grandfather died in 1773, the composer always imagined that his huge talents had come to him from his much revered namesake—himself the son of a baker in the Flemish city of Mechelen—who had become *Kapellmeister*, music director, of the Bonn court of Maximilian Friedrich in 1761. Beethoven's father, Johann, was for many years a tenor in the court choir; he taught singing and was a passably accomplished pianist and violinist as well, but at the time his father died in 1773, Johann's career was languishing and seemed unlikely to catch fire in the foreseeable future. His wife, born Maria Magdalena Keverich, the daughter of a cook at Maximilian Friedrich's summer palace at Ehrenbreitstein, already had been widowed when she married Johann in the autumn of 1767, a few days before her twenty-first birthday. A son by her first husband had died in infancy; so had her second child, Ludwig Maria, who died six days after his birth in 1769, the year before the third child, also named Ludwig, was born.

Maria van Beethoven was intelligent, patient, kind, and, it appears, utterly unassuming, the young family's critical counterpoint to Johann, who grew increasingly bombastic, erratic, and undependable following his father's death and the denial of his application to succeed him as *Kapellmeister*, his behavior later exacerbated by a severe dependence on drink. If Maria was her young son's ready support, Johann, according to the few accounts that exist, often was a terror to the boy, bullying him, beating him on occasion as well as, legends contend, dragging the weeping five-year-old from his bed to the piano late at night and drunkenly compelling him to practice.

Yet his father's rages and overbearing demeanor somehow never soured the boy on music, and his remarkable talents quickly emerged despite them. Young Ludwig was only seven when he gave his first public performance on the piano; at eight, he began to receive piano, violin, and viola instruction from a series of noted court musicians, and by age eleven he had become deputy to court organist Christian Gottlob Neefe, who had taken the boy under his tutelage a year before. Beethoven, whose academic education already had ended, occasionally played the organ at masses and court functions when

Neefe had to be absent, and the tutor was far from reluctant to heap praise on his young protégé. At Neefe's urging, the editors of the German *Magazin der Musik* posted a notice in March 1783 heralding Beethoven as a boy of "most promising talent. He plays the clavier very skillfully and with power [and] reads at sight very well. . . . This young genius deserves a subsidy in order to enable him to travel. He will surely become a second Mozart if he continues as well as he has begun."

It remains unclear whether it was Neefe or someone else who arranged four years hence for Beethoven to visit Vienna, seat of the Hapsburg throne, the capital of the Holy Roman Empire, and the locus also of Europe's cultured passion for music. Neefe—rather more in the mold of Beethoven's grandfather than his father—was kind, cultivated, and well-read, as well as being a multitalented musician, and he presumed that further training in Vienna, plus a more general sort of exposure to its rarefied musical climate, would transform the sixteen-year-old's prodigious talents into mature renown. Neefe even had hoped privately that the boy might secure an apprenticeship with Wolfgang Mozart, but it appears instead that the Austrian master—who would be dead in only four more years—heard the young man play on solely a single occasion.

Mozart's initial reaction on an April afternoon to the selection the boy from Bonn had prepared for him was decidedly cool—surely there were dozens of young fellows in Vienna who could master a single showy piece. But when Beethoven begged to be given a theme on which he might improvise, Mozart acquiesced and soon was astonished by the teenager's range and inventiveness and the power with which he played.

The young Beethoven still seemed beguiled by the music he was drawing out of the master's piano when Mozart finally walked out of the room and eagerly spoke to a group of courtiers whom he had kept waiting: "Keep your eyes on that one," he instructed. "Someday he will give the world plenty to talk about."

Beethoven might have met Mozart again; he might even have studied with him for a time, but his sojourn in Vienna was abruptly cut short by news from Bonn that his mother was gravely ill. He was able to reach her bedside before she succumbed to tuberculosis, but her death was a terrible blow to the whole family. Beethoven's infant sister, Maria Margaretha, died a few months later; two younger brothers now were left in Ludwig's care, and his father—now without his wife's hardy support and moderating influence—simply drank himself into a personal and professional collapse. When Johann was forced to resign his modest position in 1789, Beethoven, who was not yet nineteen, successfully petitioned the court to grant him half his father's former salary to help him keep the clan from destitution, becoming in the process the actual head of the household.

But although he now had to attend carefully to family matters, Beethoven nonetheless also began to blossom socially in the years that followed his mother's death. He continued to play viola in the orchestras of the court chapel and court theater, forging lasting friendships with other young musicians. He met Count Ferdinand Waldstein, eight years his senior, a music devotee to whom he became closely attached. And it was within the bonds of the prominent, progressive, and intellectually curious Breuning family, headed by the dynamic young widow Hélène von Breuning, that Beethoven first was exposed to a kind of *joie de vivre* that always had been missing in his own home. He became so closely tied to the Breunings that he often even slept at their home, and along the way he became something of a beloved stepchild to Frau von Breuning: she nursed him through bouts of illness, helped battle his recurrent black moods and sieges of brooding silence, and did her best to buoy up the self-confidence of the young man who at times was paralyzingly shy.

It was Frau von Breuning, as well as Count Waldstein and Neefe, who introduced the young man to the thrilling new notions of reform, freedom, and brotherhood—the *Aufklärung*, or Enlightenment—that were becoming common conversation pieces in the cities that flanked the Rhine and throughout much of central Europe. Yet it was Waldstein who now did the most to nurture Beethoven's musical development. He discreetly provided financial support to the young man whom he openly labeled a musical genius; he commissioned him to compose the music for his own production of a folk ballet; and he was a member as well of a larger group of the Bonn nobility who commissioned Beethoven to compose two cantatas commemorating the death of the much-loved Emperor Joseph II and the elevation of his successor, Leopold II. Although neither cantata was performed, Waldstein nonetheless recognized their brilliance. It is probable that it was he who pressed the *Joseph Cantata* into the hands of composer Franz Joseph Haydn during his visit to Bonn in 1792 in an effort to convince him to tutor young Beethoven once he was at home in Vienna again, and it is certain that it was Waldstein who convinced his friend Bonn Elector Maximilian Franz, Friedrich's successor, both to pay for Beethoven's journey to Vienna and to support him while he remained in temporary residence there.

The revolution in France that had commenced three years before by now had led to rumors of war across much of Europe. The new French regime had declared war on Austria; French forces already had reached the Rhine, and Beethoven—despite his father's failing health—had to hurry to leave Bonn if he were to be relatively assured of safe travel by coach to Vienna. As he departed, he received enthusiastic farewells from dozens of friends and admirers, all of whom anticipated his return to his hometown before too long a time, and in an album filled with their written good wishes was included this message from his devoted patron:

DEAR BEETHOVEN: You are going to Vienna in fulfillment of your long-frustrated wishes. The Genius of Mozart is still mourning and weeping over the death of her pupil. She found a refuge but no occupation with the inexhaustible Haydn; through him she wishes once more to form a union with another. With the help of assiduous labor you shall receive: *Mozart's spirit from Haydn's hands.* YOUR TRUE FRIEND, WALDSTEIN.

THE BOY WHO SNIPPED THE LOCK

IT WAS NOT UNTIL 1871 that *Kapellmeister* Ferdinand Hiller, the corpulent dean of music in the Rhine-side city of Cologne, first described for fascinated German readers what it had been like to meet Ludwig van Beethoven and what, in fact, the circumstances of the master composer's final days had been. "I can scarcely blame myself, much as I regret it, for not taking down more extended notes than I did," sixty-year-old Hiller wrote. "Indeed, I rejoice that a lad of fifteen years who found himself in a great city for the first time was self-possessed enough to regard *any* details. [But] I can vouch with the best conscience for the perfect accuracy of all that I am able to repeat."

Ferdinand Hiller had made the snow-slowed journey from Weimar to musical, magical Vienna with his piano and composition instructor, Johann Nepomuk Hummel, in the early spring of 1827 because Hummel had heard the now far-flung news that his old friend and musical rival was dying. He had wanted to see and embrace Beethoven again before he was gone, and too, he had hoped his talented protégé might be inspired by at least a few minutes spent in the company of incontestable greatness. Beethoven had received the two men warmly on March 8 and had satisfied them that their company would be efficacious in fact; they stayed with him for hours that day, then returned three more times during the succeeding fortnight before Beethoven finally succumbed to a diseased liver and a life of relentless pain. Yet on that first day, Hiller remembered, the dying man still had seemed very much alive:

Through a spacious anteroom in which high cabinets were piled with thick, tied-up parcels of music, we reached—how my heart beat!—Beethoven's living-room, and were not a little astonished to find the master sitting in apparent comfort at the window. He wore a long, gray sleeping-robe and high boots reaching to his knees. Emaciated by long and severe illness, he seemed to me, when he arose, of tall stature; he was unshaven, his thick, half-gray hair fell in disorder over his temples. The expression of his features heightened when he caught sight of Hummel, and he seemed to be extraordinarily glad to see him. The two men embraced each other most cordially. Hummel introduced me. Beethoven showed himself extremely kind and I was permitted to sit opposite him at the window. . . .

[In order for him to carry on a conversation,] thick sheets of ordinary writing paper in quarto form and lead pencils lay near him at all times. How painful it must have been for the animated, easily impatient man to be obliged to wait for every answer, to make a pause in every moment of conversation, during which, as it were, thought was condemned to come to a standstill! He always followed the hand of the writer with hungry eyes and comprehended what was written at a glance instead of reading it. . . . The conversation at first turned, as usual, on domestic affairs—the journey and sojourn, my relations with Hummel, and matters of that kind. Beethoven asked about Goethe's health with extraordinary solicitude and we were able to make the best of reports, since only a few days before the great poet had written in my album.

Concerning his own poor state, poor Beethoven complained much. "Here I have been lying for four months," he cried out, "one must at last lose patience!" Other things in Vienna did not seem to be to his liking and he spoke with the utmost severity of "the present taste in art" and "the dilettantism that is ruining everything." Nor did he spare the government, up to the highest levels. . . . "Little thieves are hanged, but big ones are allowed to go free!" he exclaimed in ill humor. He asked about my studies and, encouraging me, said, "art must be propagated ceaselessly," and when I spoke of the exclusive interest in Italian opera that then prevailed in Vienna, he gave utterance to the memorable words, "It is said *vox populi, vox dei.* I never believed it."

On March 13, Hummel took me with him a second time to Beethoven. We found his condition to be materially worse. He lay in bed, seemed to suffer great pains, and at intervals groaned deeply despite the fact that he spoke much and animatedly. . . . He also begged of Hummel to bring his wife to see him; she had not come with us, for she had not been able to persuade herself to see in his present state the man whom she had known at the zenith of his powers. A short time before, he had received a present of a picture of the house in which Haydn was born. He kept it close at hand and showed it to us. "It gives me a childish pleasure," he said, "the cradle of so great a man!"

Shortly after our second visit, the report spread throughout Vienna that the Philharmonic Society of London had sent Beethoven £100 in order to ease his sickbed. It was added that this surprise had made so great an impression on the poor man that it had also brought physical relief. When we stood again at his bedside on the 20th, we could deduce from his utterances how greatly he had been rejoiced by this altruism, but he was very weak and spoke only in faint and disconnected phrases. "I shall, no doubt, soon be going above," he whispered after our greeting. Similar remarks recurred frequently. In the intervals, however, he spoke of projects and hopes that were destined not to be realized. Speaking of the noble conduct of the Philharmonic Society and in praise of the English people, he expressed the intention, as soon as matters were better with him, to undertake the journey to London. "I will compose a grand overture for them, and a symphony." Then too, he told Frau Hummel, who had joined her husband that day, that he would visit her and go to I do not know how many places. His eyes, which were still lively when we saw him on our previous visit, were closed now, and it was difficult from time to time for him to raise himself. It was no longer possible to deceive one's self—the worst was to be feared.

Hopeless was the picture presented by the extraordinary man when we saw him again on March 23rd. It was to be the last time. He lay, weak and miserable, sighing deeply at intervals. Not a word fell from his lips; sweat stood out on his forehead. His handkerchief not being conveniently at hand, Hummel's wife took her fine cambric handkerchief and dried his face again and again. Never shall I forget the grateful glance with which his broken eyes looked upon her.

ON A MONDAY EVENING THREE days hence, Hiller and both Hummels were dining at the home of friends when additional guests arrived with the woeful news that Beethoven had died in the midst of the sudden afternoon storm. When Hummel and the boy returned to the lodging called the *Schwarzspanierhaus*, the "Black Spaniard's House," on Tuesday to pay their final respects, the face of the man whom Hummel loved and young Hiller newly was in awe of appeared strangely changed. Beethoven's body still lay in his bedroom, but now had been placed in an oak coffin that stood on a brass bier, his head resting on a white silk pillow. His long hair had been combed and was crowned with a wreath of white roses, but his grizzled visage had gone blue and the sides of his face were oddly sunken because at autopsy that morning the temporal bones surrounding his ears—as well as small bones of the ears themselves—had been removed for future study.

The autopsy had been performed by Dr. Johannes Wagner, a pathologist and associate of Beethoven's final physician, Dr. Andreas Wawruch, who had assisted him. During the methodical morning procedure, the two men had discovered that Beethoven's liver, shrunk to half the size of a healthy one, was leathery and covered with nodules; the spleen was black and tough and twice its normal size; the pancreas too was unusually large and hard; and each of the pale kidneys contained numerous calcified stones. The deaf man's auditory nerves were shriveled and marrowless, but the nearby facial nerves were impressively large; the auditory arteries were "dilated to more than the size of a crow's quill" and had become surprisingly brittle; the bone of the skull was strangely dense, and the remarkably white and fluid-filled convolutions of the brain were much deeper, wider, and more numerous than the physicians would have expected them to be. The two doctors had not been surprised, of course, when they encountered much that was abnormal, but knowledge of both pathology and disease etiology remained limited enough in that era that neither man could infer from the findings what might have caused the composer's deafness or indeed any of his many other maladies.

Because of the trauma induced by the autopsy itself, as well as the disfigurement of his face caused by the missing bones, Beethoven appeared only suggestive of the man with whom Hummel and Ferdinand Hiller had conversed a few days earlier, and the two men did not remain for long beside his coffin. But before they departed, young Hiller asked his mentor whether he might be permitted to cut a lock of the master composer's hair. It was a request that Hiller would choose not to mention in his 1871 recollection—perhaps reluctant to detail or acknowledge it, even half a century later, because throughout his life the otherwise open and gregarious Hiller virtually never had spoken about his private life or what he secretly held dear, but perhaps also because explicit permission to take a keepsake had not been granted by Beethoven's brother Johann, by Stephan von Breuning, who had become executor of his estate, or even by the factotum Anton Schindler. Yet other locks of hair, it was obvious, had been cut already, and it is easy to imagine Hummel whispering his assent to his student, the two men quietly moved by the simple ritual and the sadness of the moment, Ferdinand Hiller wielding the scissors he had brought with him for that hopeful purpose, lifting a thick lock of Beethoven's long and half-gray hair, pulling it away from his head, and setting it free.

———

FERDINAND HILLER HAD BEEN BORN in Frankfurt in 1811, the son of a wealthy merchant who, in order to help conceal his Jewish identity at a time when anti-Semitism was rising perilously in Europe, had changed his name late in the eighteenth century from Isaac Hildesheim to Justus Hiller. Yet Frankfurt itself was a comparatively tolerant city, one in which Jews, despite a few significant limitations, were able to live free from persecution. Ferdinand's father and his wife, Regine Sichel Hiller, were well-to-do, urbane, and cultivated; they were committed to doing everything they could to assimilate their son into Germany's cultural mainstream, but they were determined as well to ensure that he truly enjoyed his childhood, trying—rather unsuccessfully as it turned out—not to draw too much early attention to his remarkable musical talents. When he was seven, they acquiesced to entreaties from friends, and agreed that the boy could become a regular student of pianist Aloys Schmitt as well as take lessons in composition from Frankfurt composer J. G. Vollweiler. Three years later, ten-year-old Ferdinand performed in public for the first time, playing Mozart's Concerto in C Minor and dazzling two musicians who were present at the recital—his parents' friends Ludwig Spohr and Ignaz Moscheles, both of whom had been colleagues of Beethoven during years they spent in Vienna. The two men insisted that the boy really must be sent to Weimar to study with *Kapellmeister* Johann Hummel, himself not only a contemporary and friend of Beethoven, but also the sole composer in Europe whose talents equaled Beethoven's, at least according to men like Spohr and Moscheles.

Warm and generous and surpassingly homely, the much loved and respected Hummel accepted few students, yet as a prodigy himself forty years before in Vienna, he had lived for two years with Wolfgang Mozart and had been his student, an extraordinarily formative experience that he now felt compelled to try to return in kind. When he met the young Hiller and heard him play the piano, he was impressed by the boy's promise, and soon after Hiller became his pupil in 1825 the two also became quite close, Hummel and his wife, Elisabeth, taking paternal charge of the thirteen-year-old on his parents' behalf, and encouraging him to expand his talents in every direction. Accordingly, they introduced him to former student Felix Mendelssohn, himself an impressive prodigy only two years Hiller's senior, as well as the celebrated poet and playwright Johann Wolfgang von Goethe. In the days before they had set out from Weimar for Vienna in the spring of 1827, Goethe had written a verse in young Hiller's souvenir album, and Beethoven had been heartened to hear Hiller's news of Goethe when he and Hummel visited him in the days before he died.

Hiller heard the venerated poet's name intoned once more at the gates of the Währing cemetery on the afternoon of Beethoven's funeral, when actor Heinrich Anschütz declared that Beethoven and Goethe long had been the foremost figures in the arts of the German-speaking world. Still only a teenager, Ferdinand Hiller had met and conversed with both of these towering men, and as he watched Hummel, his portly friend and wonderful teacher, throw three laurel wreaths onto the closed coffin that now lay deep in the earth, it seemed to the young man—the lock of hair he had claimed safely tucked away in his album—that a life lived richly in the arts surely was all that he should strive for.

FERDINAND HILLER HAD RETURNED TO Weimar again in July when he read in the *Abendzeitung*, published in Dresden, an obituary written by poet and historian Johann Sporschil that described an aspect of Beethoven that the boy had not been fortunate enough to glimpse:

No longer will the citizens of friendly Vienna . . . see him hurrying through the street with his short yet firm steps barely touching the ground, until, fast as lightning, he vanishes around the corner. No longer will they be able to whisper with benevolent and indulgent pride to one another: "Did you see? Beethoven!"

Yes, Hiller *had* seen him, and he even had captured a lock of the great composer's hair. The memento had been part of Beethoven; it was neither his flesh nor his blood but it *was* him nonetheless. For many years, his wild hair had been the physical thing that most immediately characterized him—it was a metaphor somehow for his eccentric ebullience, his utter unpredictability, his astonishing artistic power—and Hiller knew he always would cherish the lock of hair and protect it vigilantly.

It may have been done while he remained in Weimar, or the task could have been completed during the months he spent at home in Frankfurt with his parents, but by the time he traveled to Paris in October 1828, Ferdinand Hiller had employed a picture framer to secure the lock of hair inside a small, oval wooden frame that had been painted black, the kind of locket in which miniature portraits commonly were displayed. The clutch of hairs—who knew how many of them there were?—had been looped into a loose coil, and protected by glass. The keepsake was now secure for those infrequent occasions when he would choose to show it to friends whom he was sure would appreciate its import, and who could be counted on to demonstrate appropriate veneration when they briefly held something of Beethoven in their hands.

Although he had just turned seventeen in 1828, Hiller's move to Paris marked his emancipation into adulthood. His parents were in hearty support of his sojourn, and they made sure as well that their son did not suffer from material wants while he was there. Unlike the young Beethoven, *Le Savant Hiller*, as he would become known, was a bona fide fellow of means—a short, dark-eyed young man whose round and expressive face evidenced an openness that drew people to him. With the revolution long over, and on the heels of the final defeat of Napoleon in 1815, the government of France had been returned to a repressive yet decidedly insecure monarchy, though faint winds of revolution still blew through the squalid, disease-plagued districts of Paris. Once again, rich and poor lived utterly separate lives in the city that now totaled a million residents, and for a moneyed immigrant like Ferdinand Hiller, it was hard to imagine a more vital and stimulating place to continue his musical training.

It did seem to Hiller, however, that Paris's musical culture possessed a single distressing flaw. Unlike the cities in Germany and Austria that he had lived in or visited by now, where the works of Ludwig van Beethoven had become very widely admired, in Paris the music of the recently deceased composer still was deemed too peculiar, too intense, too "difficult" somehow, and only recently had begun to be performed at all. Yet early in the winter of 1829, Hiller met a twenty-five-year-old French musician who was utterly determined to set his countrymen straight and to enlighten them at long last about "this inconceivable product of the most somber and reflective genius." Hector Berlioz had been born in La Côte-Saint-André, and had moved to Paris six years before to study medicine as well as music; he was a young man with a wild laugh who always seemed to be filled to overflowing with energy and the most public kinds of passion, and Hiller quickly was captivated by him personally as well as by his stalwart advocacy of Beethoven and his music. "I do not think that anyone could have met Berlioz without being struck by the extraordinary expression of his face," Hiller later wrote in a memoir. "The high forehead, precipitously overhanging the deep-set eyes, the great curving hawk nose, the thin, firmly cut lips, the rather short chin, the enormous shock of hair. . . . Whoever had once seen this head could never forget it."

That Hiller, in turn, actually had been in Beethoven's presence—that he had sat with him and heard him speak, and even
had snipped a lock of his hair—was almost too wonderful to
imagine for Berlioz, and the two men soon became fast
friends. Berlioz ardently believed that Germanic culture was
more enlightened, more forward-thinking than his own, and
he was therefore eager to attach himself to Hiller, despite the
fact that this particular German was still a teenager who remained naive about the world's perils and its pleasures. Berlioz
delighted in shocking his new friend with grisly tales from the
hospital morgue where he had studied, and he did his best to
educate him too about the pleasures of amorous love, making
Hiller his ready confidant and writing him impassioned notes
about his particular longing for Irish actress Harriet Smithson,
whom he recently had seen onstage, then subsequently had
met. "My dear Ferdinand!" he pleaded on one occasion. "Can
you tell me what is this overwhelming power of emotion, this
faculty for suffering that is killing me? . . . I have spent some
time drying the floods that have fallen from my eyes—while I
saw Beethoven looking at me with severity. . . . Truly: I am a
most unhappy man."

It was a curious notion to think that Beethoven might be
watching down on him like a god and judging whether, in
fact, young Berlioz's desire for a young woman's affections
warranted his tormented emotions. Yet that was the degree to
which he imagined his hero's omnipotence as well as the transcendent mastery his music held over those who opened themselves to it. And Berlioz, as it happened, was not alone in
believing that the posthumous Beethoven somehow could

intervene in contemporary lives. For many young artists and writers as well as musicians, the world truly had turned during the years of the Napoleonic wars and their aftermath; long-standing ideas and classical forms of expression had gone sour and stale, had become irrelevant in fact, their places subsumed by a new artistic and intellectual current that was characterized by devotion to nature, to emotion and imagination, as well as a conscious rebellion against established rules and conventions. Who better than Beethoven exemplified Romanticism, this vital and thrilling new means of artistic expression? And what better place was there than Paris for young people committed to this new form of self-expressive—and often self-absorbed—artistic passion to gather in support, mutual encouragement, and revelry? By the time Hiller arrived there, so many young Romantic artists had established themselves in the genteel as well as bohemian environs of Paris that a name, *Les Jeunes France*, had been applied to them.

"The Young France" included writers such as Victor Hugo, Honoré de Balzac, George Sand, and the German poet Heinrich Heine; artists such as Eugène Delacroix; and among the many musicians for whom Paris now had become the epicenter of Romantic innovation were Polish-born pianist and composer Frédéric Chopin, Hungarian Franz Liszt, Italian Vincenzo Bellini, as well as Berlioz. Collectively, *Les Jeunes France* comprised a cultural elite, one capable of appreciating what less sensitive, less *romantic* minds could not. "The other day I heard one of the late quartets of Beethoven . . ." Berlioz wrote to his sister Nanci, "there were nearly three hundred persons present, of whom six found ourselves half-dead through the truth of the emotion we had experienced, but we six were the only ones who did not find his composition absurd, incomprehensible, barbarous. He rose to such heights that our breath began to fail us. . . . This is music [only] for him or for those of us who have followed the incalculable flight of his genius."

Although Luigi Cherubini, director of the Paris Conservatory, was skeptical about whether Beethoven truly deserved his swelling reputation, he nonetheless had played a key role in finally bringing Beethoven's music before the French public. The conservatory had sponsored the French premiere of the *Eroica* Symphony a few months before Hiller had arrived in Paris, and that successful concert soon had been followed by a performance of the Fifth Symphony that left the cognoscenti among its listeners *foudroyé*, thunderstruck, as Berlioz remembered it. But the public performances of the great symphonies were far from common events, and it was at salons hosted by the musicians and artists themselves, as well as by their wealthy benefactors, that Beethoven's chamber music regularly was performed, analyzed, and profusely praised. It was a mark of Hiller's charm and genial good humor as much as of his financial wherewithal that his own monthly salon became an eagerly sought-after invitation, particularly when his mother Regine moved to Paris in 1833 for the manifest purpose of helping her son make the evenings spent at their home decidedly memorable ones. They were lavish nights, replete with food, drink, animated conversation, and the impassioned playing of music—evenings as well, no doubt, when a lock of hair in a black wooden frame sometimes was passed from hand to grateful hand.

Paris was such a feast of art and pleasures, in fact, that Hiller insisted that his friend Felix Mendelssohn, who had remained in Germany, come take part in it, and beginning in December 1831, Hiller, Chopin, Liszt, and Mendelssohn formed a showy Parisian foursome for a time, playing together regularly at both concerts and salon recitals, as well as spending hours each day at a favorite sidewalk café on the Boulevard des Italiens, eating pastries, playing chess, and talking endlessly. Mendelssohn recounted for his new friends and for Hiller how, in the spring of 1830, he had visited Goethe at his home in Weimar, and at the aging poet's insistence had played for him a survey of the great music of the age. Although Goethe had acknowledged Beethoven's artistic genius when they had met in Teplitz eighteen years before, the true pleasures of his work always had escaped him, and in this private music-appreciation class led by the young man whom he saw as a kind of surrogate grandson, Goethe had hoped simply to skip over the composer whom his visitor believed was the most important of them all. "He wanted nothing to do with Beethoven," Mendelssohn explained, feigning shock, "but I told him I could not let him escape, and played the first part of the [Fifth] Symphony in C Minor. It had a singular effect on him. At first he said, 'this arouses no emotion; nothing but astonishment; it is grandiose.' He continued grumbling in this way, but after a long pause he began again. 'It is very great; quite wild; it makes one fear that the house might fall down.'"

The three who heard the story delighted in the notion that brave Mendelssohn had made a Beethoven convert of the great bard of the German-speaking world. But Chopin, "Little Chopinetto," as the others called him, actually shared some of Goethe's misgivings about Beethoven's might. Chopin certainly was the most quiet, even introverted member of the Paris four-some, his health already poor when he moved to the city from Warsaw in 1831, his demeanor fastidious and in every way re-served. Effusive and fiery expressions—whether musical or oth-erwise—plainly repulsed him, and he did everything he could to avoid the constant emotional theatrics of men like Hector Berlioz. He was a Romantic who disliked Romanticism, Franz Liszt explained years later when he described his by-then-deceased colleague's uncertainties about the cult of admiration they had built around the Viennese composer.

For his part, the pallid but dashing Liszt—his face arrestingly handsome and expressive, his dark hair chopped in a severe line below his ears—belonged, like Berlioz, at the head of the queue of true-believers. A native of Hungary, he had lived in Paris for more than a decade by now and in that time had es-tablished himself as a spectacularly innovative pianist, one for whom the performance difficulties imposed by Beethoven's compositions only served to highlight his own virtuosity. "For us musicians," Liszt averred, "Beethoven's work is like the pil-lar of cloud and fire that guided the Israelites through the desert." It was a path that Hiller and his comrade musicians were keen to adhere to; for them it represented not only a col-legial appreciation of Beethoven's certain genius, but also a vi-sion of the shape their own careers as composers might take in the years to come. Writing symphonies or string quartets or piano pieces was taxing and time-consuming work, however—it depended on a kind of daily drudgery as much as it did on inspiration. Both Mendelssohn and Hiller had the luxurious means to live and work anywhere that best suited them, and early in 1836 Mendelssohn, already home again in Germany, convinced Hiller, now nearly twenty-four, that despite his flourishing friendships, his growing reputation as an organ instructor, and the flattering esteem he earned from his renowned and highly favored salon, it was time, nevertheless, for him to focus his energies on composition, to "leave the Parisian atmosphere of glory and pleasure and move into the working quarters."

LUDWIG VAN BEETHOVEN NEVER JOURNEYED to England, as he long had hoped he would, nor did he ever return to the broad valley of the Rhine where he had been raised. But the lock of his long hair that had been cut from his corpse by Ferdinand Hiller had become remarkably peripatetic by 1844. It had traveled in Hiller's careful company first to Frankfurt and Weimar in Germany, to pleasure-laden Paris where it had remained for six years, then it joined the young composer in his nearly annual moves back to Frankfurt, on to Milan, to Frankfurt once more, then to Leipzig before returning to Italy—to Florence and Rome this time—then to Frankfurt again, then again to Leipzig, and finally to Dresden, where at last Hiller slowed his march and settled for three years. Since his departure from Paris, Hiller had been in search of a stable and long-term artistic position, attempting as best he could to transform himself from child prodigy and adolescent savant into a musician of mature renown. But for reasons that seemed to have more to do with poor luck and unfortunate timing than with particular deficiencies on his part, he had yet to find the job he wanted, and without the kind of security that his friend Felix Mendelssohn had achieved in Leipzig— where he had become director of the renowned Gewandhaus Orchestra—it seemed to Ferdinand Hiller that he had little choice but to go wherever fresh opportunities led him.

Hiller had held numerous short-term musical positions in Frankfurt and Rome during the 1830s; in Milan, he had directed the rather wanly received production of *Romilda*, his first opera, and in Leipzig he had overseen a hugely successful production of the oratorio he titled *The Destruction of Jerusalem*. He had replaced Mendelssohn in 1841 while his friend spent a hiatus in Berlin, but during that year in which Hiller had managed the Leipzig orchestra, a calamitous but unexplained rift had developed between him and Mendelssohn. Neither man would describe the details of what had gone so awry between them—it was a quarrel caused by "social, not personal, sensitivities," Hiller only would say—and each remained unwilling to repair the twenty-year-old relationship without first receiving a sign of apology from the other.

During a sojourn in Italy the year before, Hiller had met and promptly married singer Antolka Hogé, a native of Poland who, because of her striking beauty, had been dubbed La Bella

Polacca by the musical press. She was a Catholic; Hiller long had been a nonpracticing Jew, and the two chose to contend with what would have been perceived as a scandalous incompatibility by becoming Protestants, a decision that was made much more for convenience than out of a shared and newfound faith. Unlike his friend Hector Berlioz, who always had been so bold, so utterly open about his romantic entanglements, Hiller, on the other hand, always had kept the details of his relationships with women rather secret. Despite his gregarious nature and his constant conviviality, Hiller was essentially private, and even his diary only obliquely refers to the likelihood that in its first years his marriage to Antolka was not an easy one. Outgoing Ferdinand continued to enjoy the companionship of female friends—relationships that his new wife always was wary of—and despite the fact that the couple would remain childless for more than a decade, Antolka quickly was forced to subsume her singing career to her husband's quest for a stable and suitably prestigious musical position, necessarily abandoning her burgeoning fame in Italy for the life of an itinerant German composer's wife.

Once they were settled in Dresden in 1844, Antolka Hiller joined her husband in establishing yet another of his storied salons, a frequent gathering of the city's artists and intellectuals that this time included composer and music critic Robert Schumann and his new wife, Clara, as well as Richard Wagner, whose dramatically innovative opera *Tannhäuser* recently had been premiered before rather puzzled Dresden audiences. The two Schumanns, like so many of Ferdinand Hiller's musical contemporaries, were ardent believers in the genius of Beethoven, and the fact that Hiller repeatedly could regale them with the tale of his deathbed visits to the master formed an important component of their budding friendship.

For his part, Wagner's passion for Beethoven even surpassed the adoration of the Schumanns, with whom he had become friends prior to their separate arrivals in Dresden in the 1840s. In much the same way in which Berlioz first had been beguiled, it had been at a Paris *Conservatoire* concert—in Wagner's case, an 1839 performance of the Ninth Symphony, which would become his lifelong obsession—when he had discovered the transcendent power of Beethoven's music. Like Berlioz, Wagner too could imagine no artistic genius greater than that which Shakespeare and Beethoven clearly had shared; and like the Frenchman as well, Wagner was spellbound:

> The effect on me was indescribable. To this must be added the impression produced on me by Beethoven's features, which I saw in the lithographs that were circulated everywhere at that time, and by the fact that he was deaf, and lived a quiet, secluded life. I soon conceived an image of him in my mind as a sublime and unique supernatural being, with whom none could compare. This image was associated in the brain with that of Shakespeare; in ecstatic dreams I met both of them, saw and spoke to them, and on awakening found myself bathed in tears.

Not only in Dresden, but in Paris as well by the 1840s, praise for Beethoven's music had become widespread. No longer was his music too avant-garde for French tastes, or for any others, nor was it his music alone that had captured people's fascination. In the nineteen years since Beethoven's death, young Romantics like Wagner, Berlioz, Liszt, the two Schumanns—and Ferdinand Hiller—had shouted that there *must* have been something supernatural about the musician himself; surely no ordinary mortal could have reached such creative heights.

IN THE DAYS IMMEDIATELY FOLLOWING the composer's death, a pyramidal headstone had been laid at his grave in the Währing cemetery, bearing only the word BEETHOVEN in capital letters. His estate had been inventoried, then auctioned—everything from manuscripts to musical instruments, from household goods to clothes and shoes. Stephan von Breuning, the executor of Beethoven's estate and his choice to become his nephew Karl's guardian, had died unexpectedly only two months after Beethoven's death, and the work of disposing of the estate—as well as the future oversight of Karl's inheritance—had gone to lawyer Jacob Hotschevar.

Anton Schindler, the factotum whom Beethoven both had needed greatly and much mistrusted, had helped himself during the days after the composer's death to four bundles of conversation books, many manuscripts and letters, Beethoven's eyeglasses and ear trumpets, a favorite clock, as well as other memorabilia—the written materials taken with Beethoven's prior permission, Schindler had contended, because they were to be passed along to Johann Friedrich Rochlitz, the longtime editor of the *Allgemeine musikalische Zeitung* and the man Beethoven had hoped would be his biographer. But when age and illness had prevented Rochlitz from undertaking the project, Schindler believed that he had had no choice but to take it on himself, producing a book alleging that he and Beethoven had worked together longer and much more amicably than they actually had, a book whose accuracy with regard to many aspects of the composer's life quickly had been called into question. The first reliable account of Beethoven's life had been published by the composer's close childhood friend Franz Wegeler a decade later. With the help of Beethoven's devoted piano pupil Ferdinand Ries, Wegeler had assembled documents, anecdotes, and impressions from a variety of sources into a "biographical note" that he had intended to be of foremost interest to people who knew the composer or to those who were passionate about his music, as well as a valuable resource for the biographer who one day would write a comprehensive life of Beethoven—a task that a young lawyer from America named Alexander Wheelock Thayer had begun to contemplate, in fact.

Almost as spellbound by Beethoven's music as the Romantic composers were, in the beginning Thayer simply had hoped to write a translation of Schindler's book for American readers, but when he had begun to compare it to Wegeler and Ries's *Notizen*, he had been struck by the many substantial discrepancies between them. In order to reconcile the two and to produce a third book that could be deemed trustworthy in every detail, Thayer now hoped to travel to Europe to initiate his own primary research for a monumental project that he would not even begin until 1849 and which, in the end, would consume the rest of his life.

Biographies of the great man were fine, as far as they went, but fierce Beethoven partisans such as Franz Liszt were convinced that a physical monument honoring him and his immortality was immediately much more important. In 1839, Liszt had come to the rescue of a group of distinguished citizens in Bonn who were working to raise the funds to erect a statue in honor of their city's native son. To aid them in their efforts, Liszt had organized and performed at a series of benefit concerts in Vienna, Paris, and London, each one featuring music by the master, and by way of expressing its thanks to him, the committee in turn requested that Liszt compose a new work that would be premiered at a gala "Beethoven Festival," the highlight of which would be the unveiling of the grand statue of Beethoven in Bonn's Münsterplatz.

In August 1845, the bronze monument, designed by renowned Dresden sculptor Ernst Julius Hähnel, was completed and in place; five thousand visitors had descended on the small city, and a high-minded and laudatory cantata composed by Liszt was ready for performance. The four-day festival was a grandly successful, if chaotic event—there were performances of the *Missa solemnis* and the Ninth Symphony as well as the cantata by Liszt; there were grand soirees and dinners and even the christening and maiden voyage of the S.S. *Ludwig van Beethoven*, which henceforth would ply the languid waters of the Rhine—culminating in the unveiling of a larger-than-life figure of Beethoven, standing high on a pedestal and wearing robes meant to make him look magisterial and more than a little otherworldly, holding a pen in one hand and a notebook in the other.

Eighty-year-old Franz Wegeler proudly was in attendance at the dedication; so too was Hector Berlioz, now feeling distressingly old at forty-one. But Frédéric Chopin declined to attend the event simply because its prospect soured his stomach. "Liszt is to call out the hurrahs in Bonn, where the Beethoven monument is to be placed," he wrote to his family in the days before the festival began. "In Bonn they are selling cigars, *véritables cigarres à la Beethoven*, who probably smoked nothing but Viennese pipes; and there already has been such a sale of old bureaus and old desks that belonged to Beethoven that the poor composer *de la symphonie pastorale* would have had to drive a huge trade in furniture." Neither was Felix Mendelssohn present, in part because his health was poor, but also because he, like Chopin, was distressed by the degree of personal showmanship he was sure Liszt would display during the four days, unfairly diverting attention from the nominal honoree. Ferdinand Hiller, who remained at home in Dresden that August, shared Chopin's concern, but he also had grown wary of Liszt for another reason—because, Hiller had heard rumblings, the bold Hungarian now made no secret of the fact that he did not like Jews.

It was difficult to believe in the beginning. The two men had reveled in each other's company during their Paris days; they had made several rendezvous in Italy, and although the many miles that physically had separated them meant that they did not see each other often, they had continued to exchange warm, if only periodic, greetings by mail. Still stung by the rupture of his friendship with Mendelssohn, Ferdinand Hiller had been determined not to lose another long-term relationship, and he had simply ignored the occasional rumors he had heard during the three years he spent as an interim music director in Düsseldorf before beginning his first heady and heartening years in Cologne—just a dozen miles down the Rhine from Bonn—where in 1850 he had been appointed the city's permanent *Kapellmeister*, the position he patiently had been in search of for the past fourteen years.

In 1851, Hiller went so far by way of reaching out to his former piano partner as to dedicate his *Études Rhythmiques* to Liszt, still the finest pianist Hiller ever had heard. A year later, Liszt returned the commendation, writing to Hiller to communicate to him "the immediate impression of your beautiful symphony that was performed tonight in our theater . . . and it is with great sincerity that I transmit to you the compliments of your public in Weimar," where Liszt now served as music director for Grand Duke Charles Alexander. Yet within months of mailing that letter, Liszt nonetheless openly assaulted Jews in general—and Hiller by implication—in his new book on Hungarian gypsies and their music, published first in France as *Les Bohémiens*, which contended that Jews lacked any creative abilities and recommended that they leave cultured Europe en masse and relocate in Palestine. Was it possible that the author of those sentiments did not know that Ferdinand Hiller, the nominal Lutheran, was Jewish? Almost certainly it was not, especially given Hiller's own assertion that he never had been "modest enough to conceal the fact that I belong to one of the world's oldest races, through which I have had the honor of enriching the city treasury every week," by paying the tariffs that then were imposed on Jews by the German government.

Although no evidence survives indicating whether Hiller read Liszt's words soon after they were published or first heard of them from perplexed friends, it is clear that their relationship did not take a dramatic downward turn until 1855, three years after *Les Bohémiens* appeared, a deterioration that began to be expressed publicly through the two men's crescendoing criticisms of each other's talents. Liszt, like Wagner, had become an avid proponent of what people had begun to call the New School, and that Liszt and his friend and confederate Richard Wagner simply liked to call "the music of the future." Beethoven's Romantic flame still burned brightly, as far as Liszt was concerned, but many of the composers who had followed him had failed the master by creating a tepid kind of music of their own that was "neither fish nor meat," as he put it, complaining as well that Hiller seemed "philosophically disinterested" in his own music or anyone else's. The bearded, balding, and by now rotund *Kapellmeister* from Cologne responded cuttingly in kind, writing a long and blistering review for the *Kölnische Zeitung*, Cologne's leading newspaper, of Liszt's performance as a composer and conductor at the 1857 Aachen Music Festival, but penning only two words about the event in his personal diary: "My Rage!"

When Wagner, now in exile in Zurich because of his radical

politics, read Hiller's assessment, he was quick to defend Liszt against what he believed had been an unwarranted attack by the "Falstaff from Cologne," a reference meant as a jab at Hiller's physical bulk as well as an ironic reminder that he was renowned for his geniality rather than his venom. Wagner himself was unconstrained by a similar reputation, and soon he wrote directly to Hiller to tell him how distressed he was to hear that Hiller recently had reestablished the music *Konservatorium* in Cologne. "Better a *Destruktorium*," he pointedly suggested, before adding that he hoped Hiller would not take his remarks too personally. It was a hope Wagner professed to cling to despite the fact that seven years earlier he had published anonymously his own diatribe against Jews, one that had preceded Liszt's racist remarks, in fact. In his 1850 book, *Jewry in Music*—which was rereleased, this time with his name attached to it, in 1869—Wagner had issued a damning indictment of the Jewish spirit and its pernicious influence on German culture. Jews, he declared, were interested in art only in order to sell it, and they were horribly detrimental to the Fatherland's cultural glory because they worked to convert the lofty realm of artistic creation into a mere marketplace. Without mentioning Hiller or anyone else by name, he lamented the fact that Jews now held important artistic positions throughout Germany, and he worried that they inappropriately influenced music and the theater in particular.

By 1870, neither Wagner nor Liszt—who lately had become Wagner's father-in-law—pretended any longer that they retained remnants of their early friendships with Ferdinand Hiller, and he, in turn, now was blunt and impassioned in his assaults on the two men's politics as well as the kinds of music they made. "Richard, the Wagnerian, [began to] hurl his anathema against the Jews from his pulpit in Switzerland some years ago . . ." Hiller wrote in the *Kölnische Zeitung*, "and now he has published a new pamphlet that is bursting with falsehood and injustice." Two years later, Hiller joked bitterly in a letter to his colleague, the conductor Hermann Levi, "You hadn't told me that you received a kiss from Wagner. It seems he wasn't afraid of the Jewish contagion!" And again in the *Kölnische Zeitung*, Hiller was acidic in his response to the newspaper's suggestion that Wagner's upcoming appearance in Cologne—where he would stage and conduct his opera *Lohengrin*—would be akin to "a bold knight [entering] the camp of declared enemies": "I cannot deny the fact the greater part of what Herr Wagner writes, composes, and does is extremely unpleasant to me," Hiller wrote. "I must nevertheless point out that I have presented his concert compositions to the public in splendid performances over the years. To see Herr Wagner conducting one of his works is something that should interest his foes and followers alike, especially since he will be using a baton for this and not his vile German prose."

FELIX MENDELSSOHN, ONLY THIRTY-EIGHT, had died suddenly in 1847 before he and Ferdinand Hiller had been able to reconstruct their long and once-vital friendship, the dissolution of which he still considered "one of the greatest losses I have had to endure in my restless life." Chopin, the man whom Hiller admitted he had fallen a little in love with when they met in wondrous Paris, had been sickly since that time and had died two years after Mendelssohn; Schumann, whose mind had betrayed him, had spent his final years in an asylum in Bonn before his death in 1856; and dear and ebullient Berlioz, once so wild and flush with life, now was gone as well. Liszt and the racist Wagner remained among the quick, and although Liszt lamely insisted that the anti-Semitic beliefs attributed to him had been inserted into his book without his approval by his longtime mistress Princess Carolyne of Sayn-Wittgenstein, and that he was a friend of many Jews, both men presently were as far from Hiller's life as he could push them. The aging Romantic now was quite alone.

Yet for twenty years Ferdinand Hiller had been the dynamic spark of Cologne's rich musical life, and he was greatly gratified by what he had accomplished. The city's music conservatory flourished now and its educational quality was heralded throughout Germany; he had established the city's monthly *Gürzenich* concerts, as well as the *Niederrheinische Musikfeste*, a summer festival, bringing Europe's finest musicians and composers to Cologne, as well as achieving there over many years what he still believed had been "my greatest joy, my greatest source of pride—to be able to conduct so many marvelous performances of the Ninth Symphony of Beethoven." During his tenure in Cologne, Hiller had become much sought-after as a visiting conductor by orchestras across the continent; he had organized and judged dozens of performance competitions; he had become a respected writer and critic, and his skills as a pianist—which first had caught the connoisseurs' attention fifty years before—still were the stuff of legend. Hiller and his wife, Antolka, it was true, never had found a way to forge a joyous marriage or a truly supportive partnership, but they had chosen to remain by each other's side nonetheless, and their Cologne salon had become as storied over the years as those gatherings they had hosted in cities elsewhere. And although Hiller virtually never wrote or spoke publicly about his family life, it is also clear that he was much adored by his son, Paul, and his daughter, Tony, both of whom had reached their early adulthoods by now and who, to his great delight, had become musicians themselves.

But at those moments when he was utterly honest with himself, Hiller also had to confess a single yet enormous disappointment: he had not become the towering composer he once believed he could be. He remembered what his beloved mentor Johann Hummel once had told him about his own efforts to achieve a certain greatness, and he wondered whether a similar fate might have befallen him. "In my opinion, Hummel would have achieved more as a composer if Beethoven's overpowering genius had not appeared right in the middle of his development like a terrible troublemaker," Hiller wrote in his book *Lives of the Artists.* " 'It was a serious moment for me when Beethoven appeared,' my master told me one day. 'Should I really attempt to follow in the footsteps of such a genius? For a long while I did not know where my place was.' " Ferdinand Hiller too had faced formidable competition along the way—his mind reeled to think of the extraordinary number of great composers whom he had counted among his friends—but now he could not help but wonder whether he too had been too slow to recognize his place. None of his six operas ever had been received enthusiastically; only one of his three symphonies had fared better; his oratorios, on the other hand, had been both popular and critical successes, and he agreed that his songs and piano pieces likely were his best work, but he remained haunted by what Mendelssohn had told him as long ago as 1837, when Hiller had begged for an honest critique: "I believe that you are now equal to any musician as far as talent is concerned, but I do not know of any piece of yours which is properly carried out." Much later, at about the time when their falling out commenced, Liszt, too, frankly had found Hiller's music wanting: "One could reproach him for not having faults, and for not giving sufficient grounds for criticism. He shows himself to be a musician who is well organized and experienced, which he is in all things, without being a master of any one of them." And before he had become mentally ill, it was Schumann who had said it all too succinctly: Hiller's music simply "lacked that triumphant power that we are unable to resist."

For the occasion of what would have been Beethoven's eightieth birthday, Hiller had composed both text and music for a cantata in his honor, performed for the first and only time at a Cologne Society Concert on the night of December 17, 1850. Two decades later, Ferdinand Hiller had proposed in a long essay—published in a special issue of the magazine *Salon* that celebrated Beethoven's centenary—precisely where the light of his genius shone most brightly. He had concluded that the fundamental brilliance of the master's music was that it achieved softness without weakness, enthusiasm without hollowness, longing without sentimentality, passion without madness. He is deep but never turgid, pleasant but never insipid, lofty but never bombastic. In the expression of love, fervent, tender, overflowing, but never with ignoble sensuality. He can be cordial, cheerful, joyful to extravagance, to excess—never to vulgarity. In the deepest suffering he does not lose himself—he triumphs over it. . . . More universal effects have been achieved by others, but none more deep or noble. No, we may say without exaggeration that never did an artist live whose creations were so truly new—his sphere was the unforeseen.

It is impossible to know whether Caroline van Beethoven, the widow of Beethoven's nephew Karl, might have read those words prior to writing to Ferdinand Hiller in March 1876. But for some reason—perhaps she knew that he once had met her late husband's celebrated uncle, perhaps it was his wealth that was renowned—it was Hiller in faraway Cologne to whom she chose to reach out for financial help. Karl van Beethoven, the composer's sole heir, had been in the Austrian military until 1832, the year in which he married. He had worked as a farm manager for two years until the death of his uncle Johann, who, like his brother Ludwig, had been childless, and who also bequeathed the whole of his estate to his nephew. The sole beneficiary of both uncles, Karl and his family had had the means to live in comfort, and Karl had not been employed again before he died in April 1858.

Following her husband's death, Caroline had been able to care for her four daughters and her son with the little capital that remained from the two estates, as well as with a stipend offered her by members of Vienna's Society of the Friends of Music. But her widowhood had not been easy: her son, named Ludwig, had been a difficult child and had grown up to be a most disreputable man—employing himself as a dealer in bogus Beethoven memorabilia, swindling a substantial sum from the king of Bavaria, to whom he had been introduced by Richard Wagner, and ending up in prison in 1872. Caroline's youngest daughter, Hermine, had suffered a long illness and almost had succumbed to the "strains of poverty," Frau van Beethoven explained in her letter to Hiller, and lately the family had fallen into desperate straits because the Society for the Friends of Music had notified her that, most regrettably, the funds for the Beethoven monument it planned to erect in Vienna were proving insufficient, and that therefore the society would have to discontinue her stipend immediately.

Ferdinand Hiller's reply to Caroline van Beethoven has not survived, but a second letter to him makes it clear that he answered her solicitation, probably suggesting that she make her difficult circumstances more widely known by making an appeal in a music journal. But such a public entreaty would prove disastrous, she explained in the second letter; family members were greatly annoyed with her for publicizing their poverty to the degree that she already had. Not for herself but for her daughter, she begged, might the kind and caring people of Bonn be able to offer assistance? Might Hiller mount a production of *Fidelio* in Cologne and pledge its proceeds to her daughter?

Hiller, it appears, turned away from her supplication at that point, neither taking it up with associates in nearby Bonn nor personally agreeing to a charitable performance on Frau van Beethoven's behalf. Hermine married in 1876, the same year in which her brother Ludwig was released from prison, at which point he abandoned his wife and six-year-old son and emigrated to America, where he worked for a time for the Union Pacific Railroad. Although poor, Caroline van Beethoven would live fifteen more years—long enough to be made a guest of honor, together with her four daughters, at the May 1880 dedication in the Vienna square renamed Beethovenplatz of a bronze statue placed in memory of a man whom she never had met, his colossal likeness seated atop a twenty-two-foot-high granite pedestal, to the base of which clung twelve angels and cherubs. Dressed in the kind of clothing he actually wore, this Beethoven looked down with the severest kind of concentration on the many thousands who had gathered below him for the august occasion, the composer depicted this time a bit more like a human being than the god Hiller and his contemporaries had believed him to be.

"I AM LIVING THROUGH MY *finale* only reasonably well," Ferdinand Hiller wrote to his friend and former pupil, the Cologne-born composer Max Bruch in November 1882. In recent years, he had been made a member of the prestigious

Berlin Academy, the University of Bonn had granted him an honorary doctoral degree, and he had been knighted as well when the Order of the Crown of Württemberg was bestowed on him. He now was the esteemed *Dr.* Ferdinand *von* Hiller, but he was also old and failing and often was depressed. "At times quite sick—at times somewhat disgruntled—I pull myself together both physically and mentally in order to go on," he continued in the letter to Bruch. "The meanness and vulgarity that, it seems, belong to the necessities of mankind are the most miserable of things." The great physical weight that Hiller had carried for so many years by now had taken a heavy toll on his heart and circulatory system, and although he continued to hold the music directorship that had been his life's focus for more than thirty years, he nonetheless suspected that his life was drawing to a close. Writing to his dear friend Johannes Brahms in Vienna, he confided one year later, "I have nothing against living a few more years. But I really hope it won't be that many."

Brahms's rejection of the so-called New School, as well as his rather unfashionable return to classical forms in his own compositions, had greatly endeared him to Hiller, and Hiller hoped that the city administrators of Cologne one day would accede to his recommendation that Brahms be named his permanent replacement. But before he left public life, Hiller worked hard to conclude it in ways he found fitting, conducting as always and still writing frequently—about music, religion, and the world of politics, which he avidly had observed throughout his life, if always from some distance.

In his book *Letters to an Anonymous Woman*, a collection of memoirs and essays presented as missives penned to a fictional woman whom he had met only in passing but had been enchanted by, Hiller confided,

You are right, dearest Madam, music and religion are the two things about which the most erroneous things have been thought, said, and written. Fortunately, our music is quite an innocent thing and is in no position to cause great damage . . . and its priests are harmless people. . . . Religion, which shares with music the fact that it is also an unsolved mystery, should imitate the latter and allow the believers to adhere to the manifestations that best suit them. . . . The advantage that music has over religion is that it is capable of uplifting and inspiring many people without having to approach reason too closely . . . [but both] are united in the task of lifting humanity above the prosaic humdrum of life—to bring hope and consolation, to transfigure grief and joy.

In *Lives of the Artists*, he wrote with great passion about the life and thought of Jewish philosopher Moses Mendelssohn, grandfather of Felix, arguing that it was scandalous that the "Jews of Berlin, both the nonconverted and the converted," had not yet erected a monument in the nation's capital in honor of the humble but brilliant man who so eloquently had insisted that it was possible indeed to be both Jewish and a patriotic German. And, of course, Hiller had been outraged beginning in 1881 when state-sanctioned pogroms perpetrated against Jews in Russia had led to increasingly violent rhetoric and scattered anti-Semitic attacks throughout eastern Europe and in Germany as well.

More than thirty years before, Hiller briefly had been elated by the promise of another revolution in France, the 1848 workers' revolt in Paris that had led once more to the establishment of a republican government. "In the space of two days, the French have propelled world history forward by fifty years," he had written at the time. "No one would have thought of the establishment of a new republic in the middle of old Europe, and certainly not so soon. How generous and magnificent is the beginning of this new era in the life of nations!" But as an old and now far more cynical man, Ferdinand Hiller no longer easily could muster optimism about the continent's political future, particularly with regard to the way in which he increasingly observed Jews being robbed of basic human rights. "A lot of water will flow down the Rhine before a Jew is given a fine funeral in Germany. I find the political and religious circumstances everywhere to be worthy of the strongest criticism," he wrote to aging Jewish theologian Berthold Auerbach shortly before Auerbach's death. "I wonder whether you and I will really miss taking part in the next fifty years. I don't think so. We will be able to travel more comfortably—maybe we will even eat and drink better—but a lot of blood will flow and men will not be human anymore," he added with chilling prescience.

On May 1, 1883, Ferdinand Hiller systematically began to put his affairs in order in preparation for the death that he sensed soon would be at hand, and the first of his final acts was to offer his son, Paul—now an opera singer with a burgeoning career like his mother once had had—a momentous gift on the occasion of his thirtieth birthday. Hiller wanted his only son to have and henceforth safeguard the locket in which fifty-six years before he had secreted the lock of Ludwig van Beethoven's hair.

Next, he retired from the position that had been his honor and great joy to hold for thirty-four years; and then, with his wife Antolka's help, he began to catalog the writing and correspondence that carefully chronicled his rich life. He began one more project, a series of essays he hoped to title *Letters from the Sick Room*, but soon his failing health precluded it. "You want to know how I'm doing," he scribbled in response to an inquiry from friend and fellow composer Carl Reinecke. "This is hard to answer. I eat, sleep, even compose a little, but in between I am plagued by such misery that I basically have little joy left in life. I haven't left my room now for more than two months."

His heart remained under enormous stress, his bladder failed, and lack of circulation caused his legs to become grossly and painfully swollen. He complained about the music—the *noise*—he heard coming from hurdy-gurdy players in the street outside his window, and friends would come on occasion to offer him the blissful sounds of violins or the songs of their voices instead, but then, in the still and dark early morning of

May 11, 1885, seventy-three-year-old Ferdinand Hiller died, his head held in his son's embracing arms.

Newspapers throughout Europe reported his passing, and obituaries noted in particular the astonishing number of great musicians with whom he had come in close contact during his long life, many of whom he had made his dear and devoted friends. London's *Musical Times* noted that "Hiller, in the records of his art, will stand high among the *dei minores*, and even within the shadow of the throne of genius—not the loftiest place, but one worth gaining surely." Following a somber memorial service held for family members in his home on May 13, Hiller's remains were carried to Cologne's Melaten Cemetery, where a Lutheran minister conducted a brief graveside service and conductor Franz Wüllner delivered what everyone in attendance agreed was a lyrical and utterly merited eulogy, Wüllner affirming that his friend had succeeded wonderfully in his lifelong commitment to countering mundanity with the exhilarating sounds of beauty, that he had devoted his life to art.

No account of the act has survived—and of course it may not have happened—but there is fitting symmetry in supposing that before he helped commit his body to the ground, Paul Hiller surely saved a lock of his famed father's hair.

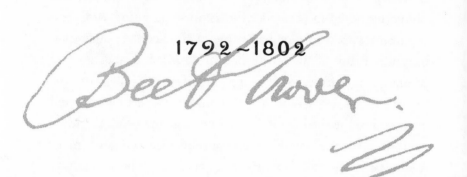

1792~1802

MUCH LIKE THE MUSIC HE made, Beethoven himself harbored stark contradictions and moods that would vacillate wildly. He was obsessive about bathing, for example, but in his later years he seemed to ignore utterly the filthy clothes that he wore. He believed in the nobility of art but also was enduringly impressed by the rather paler nobility that was bestowed by social class. "You will see that I have become a first-rate fellow," he had boasted in a letter to Franz Wegeler, his boyhood friend from Bonn who was then a medical student. "Not only as an artist but also as a man you will find me better and more fully developed." But the fellow whom Wegeler had encountered when he visited Vienna had proved as capable of being irascible, self-obsessed, tactless, and petty as he sometimes was at demonstrating overwhelming kindness, the most stalwart sort of friendship, and a ready, still-boyish sense of humor. In addition, Beethoven repeatedly fell in love with women whose marriages or social positions had made actual and authentic relationships with him impossible, yet rather simpler friendships with females were often difficult for him. The close companion whom he repeatedly had labeled a "false dog" would become, just as certainly, his "Dear Little Ignaz of my Heart" within a day or two each time. Yet this man of many tempers and diverse opinions also was capable of recognizing his contradictions and bountiful shortcomings, confessing to them as readily as he occasionally acknowledged his genius. "It is a peculiar feeling," he once had allowed to his close friend, the violinist and theologian Karl Amenda, "to see and hear oneself praised and at the same time to realize one's own inferiority as fully as I do."

Surely some of Beethoven's petulant temperament—or even the lion's share of it, in fact—was explained by his perennially poor health. While still an adolescent, he had begun to be battered by bouts of gastrointestinal disease, and in maddening progression over the succeeding years he also had suffered intense headaches, a series of virulent abscesses and infections, pneumonia, and bronchitis. At sixteen, soon after he was recalled from Vienna to his mother's deathbed, he had contracted a sudden fever accompanied by labored breathing, and the two maladies had been succeeded by what he labeled a melancholia, and which surely could have been attributed to

her death. By the time he settled in Vienna in 1792, he peri-
odically was plagued with the abdominal pain, cramping,
constipation, and diarrhea that then was labeled *kolik*. He suffered a prolonged bout of this "colic" in 1795; then in 1797 "a
terrible typhus" befell him, an illness that likely was a severe,
disorienting fever. When at last he confessed his failing hearing in an 1801 letter to Franz Wegeler, who now was a prac-
ticing physician in Bonn, his whole health appeared to be
collapsing:

For the last three years my hearing has become weaker
and weaker. The trouble is supposed to have been caused
by the condition of my abdomen, which, as you know,
was wretched even before I left Bonn, but has become
worse in Vienna, where I have been constantly afflicted
with diarrhea and have been suffering in consequence
from an extraordinary debility. . . . During this last winter
I was truly wretched for I had dreadful attacks of *kolik* and
again relapsed completely into my former condition. . . .
In order to give you some idea of this strange deafness, let
me tell you that in the theater I have to place myself quite
close to the orchestra in order to understand what the
actor is saying, and that at a distance I cannot hear the
high notes of instruments or voices. As for the spoken
word, it is surprising that some people have never noticed
my deafness; but since I have always been liable to fits of
absentmindedness they attribute my hardness of hearing
to that. Sometimes too I can scarcely hear a person who

speaks softly; I can hear sounds, it is true, but I cannot make out the words. But if anyone shouts, I can't bear it. Heaven alone knows what is to become of me.

For the time being, Beethoven confided only in Wegeler in Bonn and his friend Karl Amenda, who had left the city on an extended journey in 1799. Except for these two distant confidants, he remained mute about his terrible new trouble and did his best to shield it from friends and colleagues at home, although it seems sadly certain that he succeeded in fooling only himself.

IT WAS IN 1797, AT THE age of twenty-six, when he had begun to miss words and then whole phrases in conversations, and he began too to hear incessant, painful, and surely deranging buzzing and ringing sounds. But four years had passed before he had been able to confess his failing hearing and to begin to seek the cure that never had come. Five months later, after Wegeler had begged for more information about his hearing loss, Beethoven again wrote to his friend, but this time with slightly better news. "My life is again somewhat pleasanter, for I am mixing more in society. You can scarcely imagine what a dreary, sad life I led during the past two years." Although his hearing had not improved, there was a very specific reason why his spirits had lifted: "This change has been brought about by a dear charming girl who loves me and whom I love. After two years I am again enjoying a few blissful moments; and for the first time I feel that marriage might bring me happiness. Unfortunately, she is not of my class, and now—for the moment I certainly could not marry—I must bravely bustle about."

Although he didn't name her, the young woman whom Beethoven was enchanted by as the year 1801 came to a close almost certainly was his seventeen-year-old piano student, Countess Giulietta Guicciardi, someone whose nobility would have made marriage to him most unlikely. And she was not, in fact, the first woman Beethoven had considered marrying—his 1795 proposal to singer Magdalena Willman quickly had been rejected—but it is clear in the letters he wrote to Countess Guicciardi that, at least briefly, Beethoven believed he finally had found someone who not only loved him but who also might make bearable his steadily diminishing hearing.

Nine months later, near the end of a sojourn in the tranquil village of Heiligenstadt not far from Vienna—where he had gone on the advice of his physician—Beethoven had grown deeply distraught not only about his advancing deafness but also his growing recognition that his relationship with a countess little more than half his age simply held no promise. On October 6, 1802, he addressed to his two brothers a long, fulminating letter that seemed intended to be at once a public confession of his terrible medical secret—a will of sorts, perhaps even a suicide note—as well as an impassioned plea for understanding. "You men who think or say I am hostile, peevish, or misanthropic," he wrote, how greatly you wrong me. You do not know the secret cause which makes me seem so to you. From childhood on, my heart and soul were full of the tender feeling of goodwill, and I was always inclined to accomplish great deeds. But just think, for six years now I have had an incurable condition. . . . Though born with a fiery, lively temperament, susceptible to the diversions of society, I soon had to withdraw myself, to spend my life alone. And yet if I wished at times to ignore all this, oh how harshly was I pushed back by the doubly sad experience of my bad hearing; and yet it was impossible for me to say to people, "Speak louder, shout, for I am deaf." Ah, how could I possibly admit weakness of the one sense which should be more perfect in me than others, a sense which I once possessed in the greatest perfection, a perfection such as few in my profession have or ever have had?

What humiliation for me when someone standing near me heard a flute in the distance and I heard nothing, or someone heard the shepherd singing and again I heard nothing. Such incidents brought me almost to despair; a little more and I would have ended my life.

Only my art held me back. Ah, it seemed to me impossible to leave the world until I had produced all that I felt was within me; and so I spared this wretched life. . . .

You, my brothers, Carl and [Johann], as soon as I am dead, if Dr. Schmidt is still alive, ask him in my name to describe my disease, and attach this written document to his account of my illness, so that at least as much as possible the world may be reconciled to me after my death. . . .

Farewell, and do not completely forget me when I am dead. I have deserved this from you, since I often thought of you during my life, and of ways to make you happy; do be so.

Still two months away from his thirty-second birthday, Ludwig van Beethoven was consumed with the melodramatic certainty that his life—or at least the life that mattered to him—was coming to a close. He had accomplished much in the decade since his arrival in Vienna: he could claim a certain personal fame among the cultured elite, a reputation as the finest pianist his adopted city ever had seen, and growing renown as a composer. His oeuvre by now included more than two dozen piano sonatas, violin sonatas, piano trios, string quartets, a piano quintet, a piano concerto, a C major symphony, as well as a new symphony in D major, on which he currently was at work. Critics were fascinated by his music, if often more than a little perplexed by it; his loyal and generous patrons, as well as the publication of his compositions, now kept him comfortable financially; friends were quick to rally to his assistance—and to his defense when required—and at long last he even had proved to himself that his charms were not entirely lost on women. Yet none of it seemed to matter as his exile in Heiligenstadt drew to a close. He had little choice, it at last seemed clear, but to return to his life in the raucous city whose sounds increasingly were lost to him and to resolve, nonetheless, to draw the music out. He confessed his terrible calamity, his awful fate, to his brothers and all the world, but then Beethoven folded the paper on which he had written his aching testament and tucked it away, showing it to no one for the remainder of his life.

A GIFT IN GILLELEJE

AUTUMN SOON WOULD GIVE WAY to winter and Cologne art dealer Hermann Grosshennig's busy Christmas season was under way in mid-December 1911 when he made time to attend to a special request. A rather formal but nonetheless congenial gentleman sporting a Kaiser Wilhelm mustache—he was a journalist and long ago was a singer, he had explained—recently had come into Grosshennig's small gallery in the Langgasse bearing a wood-frame locket roughly as big around as an apple. The locket held tight two pieces of glass and between them was a lock of hair shaped into a coil. The man's father had placed the hair in the locket eighty-four years before, back when he was still a boy, and after nearly a century of being passed from hand to hand, it now needed a bit of repair. Grosshennig made frames for the artwork he sold, and yes, he assured the man, he could reseal and restore the locket. The hair inside it was Beethoven's, the man had told him. He was certain it had belonged to the great composer because his own father had cut it, and his father had been Cologne's beloved *Kapellmeister* Ferdinand Hiller, whom Grosshennig remembered, of course.

When Paul Hiller, now fifty-eight, returned the week before Christmas to the gallery that lay in the long shadow of the *Dom*—Cologne's enormous, twin-spired Gothic cathedral— the locket was ready to be collected as promised, and it seemed to be prepared as well for another eighty years of service. The two pieces of glass were cleaned and polished, and the edges where they touched had been sealed together with glue; the wooden frame was freshly painted, and it too had been sealed with brown backing paper. But the craftsman had done one more thing, he explained to the locket's owner, and he hoped Herr Hiller would not object: beneath the outer backing was a similar layer of paper on which Grosshennig had written, "Newly pasted to make it dust-free. Original condition improved. Cologne d.18/12 1911." He had signed his name as well, he said, because a cherished relic such as this deserved careful documentation, and also because it meant very much to him to have drawn so near to Beethoven, even if only briefly and in a manner so simple.

It is impossible to know—because, unlike the frame maker, he did not date the words he wrote—but presumably it was also during that holiday season of 1911 when Paul Hiller made his own inscription on the brown paper that was visible on the locket's underside: "This hair was cut off Beethoven's corpse by my father, Dr. Ferdinand v. Hiller on the day after Ludwig van Beethoven's death, that is, on 27 March 1827, and was given to me as a birthday present in Cologne on May 1, 1883." Grosshennig had been correct, Hiller recognized: it made good sense to document what treasure the locket contained, particularly because the incredibly curious prize his locket held was a palpable bit of Ludwig van Beethoven himself.

PAUL HILLER HAD BEEN THIRTY years old when his father—just two years away from his death—had presented him with the locket that held the hair. It was a gift that might have been made to his sister, Tony, three years his elder and an accomplished musician herself, but likely it had seemed more fitting to the elderly Ferdinand Hiller to pass Beethoven's fragile remains to his only son.

Born in Paris in 1853 during his parents' brief holiday there, Paul Hiller had become a professional singer—like his mother before him—by the time of his thirtieth birthday, a baritone in the city opera at Chemnitz, near Dresden. Although there is no record of him being married at that time, he also was the father of a one-year-old son, Felix Ferdinand, who was born in Chemnitz in 1882. Nineteen years after the gift of the locket—when Paul Hiller was forty-nine—he had returned to live in Cologne again, and he finally had married in 1902.

Little is known about his wife, Sophie Lion, except that, like her husband, she was both a Jew and a professional singer, and that soon she bore him two more sons, Edgar Ferdinand, born in May 1906, and Erwin Ottmar, born in April 1908.

A year after his marriage, Paul Hiller was appointed music critic of Cologne's *Rheinische Zeitung*, a newspaper position he would hold for twenty-four years, reviewing over the course of a quarter century virtually every operatic and orchestral performance scheduled throughout the lower Rhineland, including the monthly *Gürzenich* concerts his father had established long ago, and the still enormously popular summer music festival that had been his father's offspring as well. It was wonderful work for someone who had been steeped in music and culture throughout his life: Paul Hiller was able to make his home in the vital, Rhine-side metropolis where he had grown up; he had the heady privilege of attending concerts for a living and subsequently speaking his mind about their delights and demerits; and he had time too to write at length about his rather more specialized musical interests. He wrote new, German-language translations of the librettos to Giuseppe Verdi's operas *Ernani, Rigoletto,* and *Il Trovatore* for the publisher Ricordi; he translated Camille Saint-Saëns's *Déjanire* into German as well; and he published two scholarly texts—*The Lieder Cycle of A. Friedrich von Hessen* in 1910, and *Old English Tunes* in 1911. Although his name is not attached to it, Paul Hiller seems certain to have been the author as well of a tribute to his father published in the *Kölnische Zeitung* on October 24, 1911, the one hundredth anniversary of Ferdinand Hiller's birth.

The elder Hiller had contributed dozens of articles and let-ters to Cologne's leading newspaper during his three-decade tenure as the city's music director, so it was fitting that it was the *Kölnische Zeitung* that chose to remember him. His son was employed by a rival newspaper, though, and the article re-ferred to him in the third person, yet both its tone and its con-tent affirm that he, in fact, was the tribute's anonymous author. Anecdotal and enormously appreciative of the breadth of Ferdinand Hiller's musical career, the short article cataloged highlights ranging from his teenage encounter with Goethe to his sad farewell from public life.

In his early years in Paris, the article recounted, Ferdinand Hiller "befriended the spiritual heroes of the time . . . [and] we recall the piquant words that Countess Platen used to address Chopin, and which so aptly characterized Hiller's personality and significance: 'My little Chopin! If I were young and merry, I would take you as my husband, Hiller as my friend, and Liszt as my lover.'" The tribute made special note of the dazzling beauty of Ferdinand's wife, Antolka, as well as her years of "prudent and skillful supervision" of Sunday concerts at the *Rheinberg* beside the river, where, together with her husband, they "assembled everyone in the city who played, thought, and strove towards music." The article noted Ferdinand Hiller's close relationships with Mendelssohn, Schumann, and Brahms; it acknowledged his distaste for the "New School" composers whose work followed theirs, and it admitted as well that he had continued to compose long after "the rest of the world had ceased to encourage him therein. . . . In later years a friend once asked him, 'What, are you still composing?' To which he

replied, 'What do you want? Composing is such a great pleasure and staved paper is so cheap!' "

The tribute also declared that Ferdinand Hiller "took with
him indelible impressions from his many visits to the dying
Beethoven" eighty-four years before, impressions that lasted
throughout his lifetime, and it confessed that the fifteen-year-
old took something else from the great man as well: "He was
allowed to cut a lock of the dead master's hair that today is in
the possession of Hiller's son, the music writer Paul Hiller of
Cologne, who guards it as a cherished legacy." Together with
the explanation he inscribed on the back of the locket, those
few words comprise the only written acknowledgments yet
discovered of the fact that Ferdinand Hiller did indeed clip a
lock of Beethoven's hair, then treasured it throughout his life.

IN THE DAYS FOLLOWING THE publication of the tribute
to Ferdinand Hiller, it is probable, given the great esteem in
which Beethoven was held, that Hiller's son Paul must have
had a flood of requests from friends, acquaintances, even
strangers wanting to see the lock of hair. This may explain why
six weeks later he chose to have the locket refurbished, or perhaps it was simply the centenary of his father's birth and the accumulated emotional weight of the great gift he had been
given that together made the time seem right for the restora-
tion. But the record grows distressingly faint at this point:
Hermann Grosshennig's inscription on the locket's inner
paper, dated just thirteen days before 1911 came to a close,

followed—presumably soon—by Paul Hiller's own explanatory note, provide the last physical evidence of the lock of hair or its whereabouts for the subsequent thirty-two years.

In only three more years, the assassination of Archduke Francis Ferdinand, heir to the Austro-Hungarian throne, would catapult all of Europe into a disastrous war; in just eight more years, the formation of the National Socialist German Workers' Party and its rapid rise to prominence would ignite the kind of organized persecution of Jews in Germany that Ferdinand Hiller fearfully had envisioned forty years before; Adolf Hitler would seize national power in twenty-two years, summarily excluding Jews from the protections of German law; and in little more than twenty-five years hence, Europe would be at war for a second time in the new century, and the Nazis' *Endlösung*, the "final solution of the Jewish problem," would be horrifyingly under way. Not only would the parochial importance of a cherished lock of hair shrink in the midst of the events that would make Europe a calamitous killing ground, but those momentous events themselves also would shape dramatically the locket's future and hold its whereabouts in dusky shadow.

In the eighty years since Hiller, Berlioz, Liszt and their musical comrades in Paris first had striven to elevate Beethoven to the status of a composer-God, love of his compositions and devotion to him as a mythic ideal had continued to swell throughout much of the world. His orchestral and chamber music had increased in popularity in each succeeding decade, despite dramatically evolving musical tastes; a series of biographies—some accurate and highly informative, others elaborately fictionalized—had been published in three languages; dozens of plays, poems, and novels, including one by the Russian luminary Leo Tolstoy, had employed the basic story of Beethoven's life as their narrative grist, and great statues in his honor had been erected in Bonn and Vienna. When his grave had fallen into disrepair in 1863, Vienna's Society of the Friends of Music successfully had petitioned for permission to exhume Beethoven's body and rebury it. Then in 1888, his body had been disturbed a second time when it was removed to the city's Central Cemetery and interred alongside the remains of Vienna-born Franz Schubert, twin headstones marking the two composers' resting places.

A year later, residents of Bonn had reminded the world that Beethoven was *their* native son when the house where he was born had been restored and made into a museum, but it was in Vienna again in 1902 when a group of avant-garde artists and musicians had ushered Beethoven's memory and music into the brave new century with a sensational "Beethoven Exhibition." Centered around the ceremonial unveiling of Leipzig sculptor Max Klinger's marble monument, which had been seventeen years in construction, the exhibition had been the brainchild of a group of young, iconoclastic Vienna artists led by painter Gustav Klimt who dubbed themselves "Secessionists." For them, Beethoven epitomized not only artistic genius but also the personal triumph of purity over base sensuality, a subject scandalously addressed by Klimt's *Beethoven Frieze*, which covered three walls of the interior of the four-year-old Secession Pavilion when the exhibition opened. Much human nakedness indeed was depicted in Klimt's frieze, and Klinger's larger-than-life Beethoven also was stripped of clothing, his modesty protected only by a swath of marble cloth. Constructed of many types of stone, as well as ivory, gold, bronze, and gems, Klinger's Beethoven was seated on a throne adorned by five angels, yet his face—patterned after a life mask made long ago by sculptor Franz Klein—was unadorned, human, and strikingly reminiscent of the man who once had lived only a block away a century before. Although renowned French sculptor Auguste Rodin had pronounced the exhibition "tragic and magnificent" following its opening on April 5—for which occasion Gustav Mahler, head of Vienna's Imperial Opera, had rescored parts of the Ninth Symphony solely for woodwinds, brass, and voices—most critics had been convinced that the great installation inside the starkly modern Secession Pavilion was nothing more than highbrow pornography, utterly unsuited to "honorable women and young maidens."

But the scandal—such as it was—had been brewed by the young Secessionists, not by Beethoven surely, a subtlety that the critics took pains to point out, and his godlike reputation had not suffered greatly or for long in Vienna or in Europe at large. The myth of the divine Beethoven had remained intact for some time longer across the Atlantic as well, where nineteenth-century transcendentalists such as Ralph Waldo Emerson and Margaret Fuller long since had convinced their like-minded countrymen in the United States that Beethoven wonderfully embodied an ideal spiritual reality capable of transcending the base and often painful physical world.

Beethoven had been dead for eight decades when Paul Hiller

refurbished the locket that held his hair. But the composer had remained vitally alive in the hearts of his adherents as the twentieth century opened, much more a god still among them than a simple man who once had lived and suffered and made extraordinary music. It wasn't until World War I had begun to soak the remnants of Romanticism in both blood and misery that the cult of Beethoven, which Ferdinand Hiller long ago had played a part in creating, at last came to a sobered close. Particularly in France and the English-speaking world, people suddenly no longer could ignore the fact that Beethoven—for all his musical genius—had been a *German*, and an enemy nation simply could not produce someone worthy of a kind of worship. The Fifth Symphony, the Ninth, the Kreutzer Sonata, and the late string quartets remained splendid music, of course. But in the horror of the fighting and its hollow aftermath, something seemed newly clear to many who once had believed starkly otherwise: the man who had created those great works had been only a man in the end.

PAUL HILLER, JOURNALIST AND MUSIC scholar, had been keenly interested over the years to read the infrequently published volumes of the monumental *Life of Beethoven* that American Alexander Wheelock Thayer had begun work on more than a half century before, a biography, unlike most of its predecessors, that had been intended to describe the composer's life as it actually had occurred. Soon after Thayer had initiated the project in 1849, he had enlisted the long-term assistance of writer and historian Hermann Deiters, whose principal task it would be to edit Thayer's writing and translate it into German, the appropriate language in which the exhaustive biography should be published, Thayer believed. The two men had succeeded in completing three volumes—addressing the composer's life through 1816—when, following years of failing health and a mounting writer's block, Thayer had died in 1897 and the task of completing the project had fallen to Deiters alone.

Deiters had been able to finish the biography's fourth volume in the weeks before to his own death in 1907, then it had fallen to his colleague Hugo Riemann to complete the fifth and final volume, to reedit its predecessors, and to oversee the publication in 1917 of the definitive, five-volume set, a biography that in the end succeeded stunningly in its scope, its scale, and its "devotion to Beethoven the *man*," as Thayer long ago had hoped it would—a work that proved to Paul Hiller and thousands of kindred Beethoven devotees that the composer had been, in fact, all the more remarkable for his flawed humanity. His was *human* music, not the work of a god of any rank, and therein lay both its mystery and its enormous, enduring appeal.

Paul Hiller, age eighty-one, white-haired, still handsome, and not at all the corpulent man his father had been, died on January 27, 1934, soon after suffering a stroke at his home at 31 Eifelstrasse in Cologne. At his bedside were his wife Sophie, her age unknown, and his two younger sons—Edgar, soon to be twenty-eight and an opera singer like his father and grandmother before him had been, and Erwin, then twenty-six and an actor, both sons still living at their parents' home. Unknown to them and residing in Berlin at the time was their half brother Felix, fifty-one, who had grown up in Chemnitz, and who had supported himself as an artist in his younger days before becoming a composer, continuing in the tradition of his paternal grandfather.

Three days after Paul Hiller's death, a paid obituary appeared in a Cologne newspaper, the small notice bearing a thick black border and headed by a simple black cross. "After a life of rich artistic creativity," it read,

> righteous up to this death, our unforgettable dear husband and father, Herr Paul Hiller, music writer, passed away unexpectedly . . . at the age of eighty-one. He died firmly believing in his Savior. In accordance with his wishes, we have laid our beloved departed one quietly to his final rest in the Southern Cemetery in Cologne. In deep sorrow: Sophie Hiller; Edgar and Erwin Hiller. We ask friends to abstain from condolence visits.

Paul Hiller had worked as a staff writer for the *Rheinische Zeitung* for a quarter century, a position he had held until eight years before, yet it was not that newspaper in which his family chose to have the obituary published. Neither did it appear in the *Kölnische Zeitung*, the periodical that had published Paul's memorial article on the centenary of his father's birth. Instead, the obituary had been purchased in the *Westdeutscher Beobachter*, and therein lay the first of many subsequent mysteries. Why did Paul Hiller's family choose to note his passing in the Cologne newspaper that was the most zealously pro-Nazi at that moment? Had Paul Hiller borne ill will toward the newspaper where he had worked so long, and was this choice therefore evidence of some spite? Or did the family members choose to publish the obituary in the *Westdeutscher Beobachter* specifically in order to help mask their Jewish identity, to protect themselves from harassment and the growing threat of violence?

Could that attempt at concealment account as well for the use of the cross and the short notice's two separate references to Paul Hiller's—and by inference his family's—devout Christianity? Ferdinand Hiller and his wife, Antolka, had become converted Lutherans almost a century before, and their son therefore was at least a nominal Christian, yet by all accounts his parents' conversion had been one only of convenience. For four generations by now, the Hildesheim family had called itself Hiller in order to help it assimilate into middle-class German society as well as circumvent the very real possibility of persecution. Were the posting of Paul's obituary in a pro-Nazi newspaper and the repeated references to his Christian faith merely the continuation of a lamentable but necessary family tradition carried out this time in frighteningly dangerous times?

THE TREATY OF VERSAILLES, SIGNED in 1919 in the aftermath of World War I, had stripped Germany of military

control of what had been Beethoven's homeland as well as its
territorial hold on his adopted country. Excluded by the vic-
torious Allied nations from participation in the Paris Peace
Conference at which Europe's new political boundaries had
been delineated, Germany had been forced to accept the de-
militarization of the Rhineland along its western border with
France. It had been Germany's humiliations in the aftermath of
World War I that had helped make the country ripe during the
1920s for the emergence of the National Socialist German
Workers' Party. Led by an obsessive Austrian immigrant named
Adolf Hitler, its members had been maniacally committed to
rebuilding Germany's military power, as well as ridding their
country of its insidious Communists, the vast majority of
whom were Jews, or so the Nazis believed.

Following the onset of a disastrous international depression
in 1929, the Nazis had argued that the depression was a
Communist plot engineered by Jewish financiers; they had
promised voters a strong Germany free of Jewish control,
good jobs, and national glory, and Nazi representation in
the German parliament had risen sharply following elections
in 1930. In January 1933, German president Paul von
Hindenburg had acquiesced to mounting pressure within the
parliament and had appointed Hitler as the nation's new chan-
cellor. A month later, the *Reichstag*, the national parliament
building in Berlin, had been burned by arsonists, and in the
fear and furor that followed that attack, which Hitler himself
may have instigated, he had been able to outlaw all political
parties but his own and to win passage of the so-called
Enabling Act, which had dissolved the republican government

and had granted to Hitler broad dictatorial powers. Soon business, labor, agriculture, education, and culture all had become subject to Nazi control, and a secret state police, the Gestapo, had been established in order to crush potential dissent and insurrection, its brutality openly aimed at Jews, who thenceforth had been removed from leading positions in all facets of German life.

In the months following Paul Hiller's death in January 1934, it remained unclear precisely how difficult life would become for Germany's Jews, but by the autumn of 1935, with the passage of the so-called Nuremberg Laws, the future had begun to grow shockingly clear: Jews now no longer could vote, they could not hold an array of jobs and professions, and property owned by Jews could legally be seized.

Throughout Germany, hundreds of thousands of Jews—including those who were converted Protestants as well as those whose parentage meant they were what the Nazis deemed "half-Jews"—now began to debate whether it would be wisest to flee the country rather than risk further persecution, although emigrating appeared as a truly feasible option only to those who had the financial means to do so, a privileged group that would have included Paul Hiller's widow, Sophie, and her sons among its numbers. Jewish writers, artists, and musicians were among the first to begin to flee their homeland, in fact, and as many as fifteen hundred of them fled specifically to neighboring Denmark beginning in 1933.

The 1934 *Adressbuch*, Cologne's city directory, listed only Sophie Hiller and her son Edgar as living in the house at

Eifelstrasse 31. It is possible, however, that Erwin, the youngest son, then twenty-seven, remained in residence there as well and simply was not listed, but by 1935, neither son's name appeared in the *Adressbuch*, although their mother did still live at her long-term home. By 1936, the city's streets now jammed with stern-visaged soldiers in the wake of the Nazis' massive remilitarization of the Rhineland, the *Adressbuch* no longer showed evidence of *any* member of the Hiller family living in Cologne, not in the leafy Eifelstrasse nor anywhere else in the great city that had been the family's home for more than eighty years.

Had Sophie Hiller fled Germany for another country where she would have believed herself more secure? Had her sons escaped as well? Had they traveled together, separately, or did they remain in Germany somehow sheltered from view? And what had become of the storied lock of Ludwig van Beethoven's hair?

Paul Hiller had contended twenty-five years before that he guarded the hair as a cherished legacy of his father, and, taking him at his word, it is difficult to imagine that he might have sold the hair or simply lost track of it sometime during the twenty-three years that followed. What seems probable is that Paul Hiller planned to pass it to one of his sons. Felix, his eldest, might have received the gift, yet he lived in faraway Berlin, and it bears noting as well that his illegitimacy probably kept him at a significant physical and emotional remove from his father if he was in contact with him at all. The next son, the singer Edgar, elder of the two sons whom Paul and Sophie shared, might have been bequeathed the locket that held the hair, but it also is very possible that it remained in Sophie's possession sometime into the future. Despite her husband's advanced age, he nevertheless died unexpectedly, and it is possible that he did so before he made known whom he wished to own Beethoven's hair.

What is wonderfully certain, however, is that the lock of hair *did* survive. Resealed inside its locket thirty-two years before, Beethoven's hair reappeared, most improbably, in the small fishing port of Gilleleje—pronounced Gill-uh-LIE-uh—on the north coast of the Danish island of Sjælland in October 1943. But how did it reach that sea-battered outpost only a few kilometers across the icy Øresund from the shores of war-neutral Sweden? And where had it and its owner resided during the years before? Had the lock of hair still remained in Germany on *Kristallnacht*, the Night of Broken Glass, when, in November 1938, brownshirted mobs broke the windows of Jewish shops, burned synagogues, and attacked Jewish citizens in the streets of Cologne and throughout all of Germany? Where were the lock of hair and its surely fear-racked owner when, ten months later, German troops invaded Poland and the Second World War dramatically was under way, Germany's borders closed and the country all but impossible to escape? How did it come to pass that a lock of hair clipped from the head of a long-dead composer was one of the few possessions carried by a refugee fleeing for his life or for hers? And if the lock of hair was carried on the escape simply because it was precious, why then did its owner subsequently give it away in Gilleleje on a cold October night?

WITHIN NINE MONTHS OF GERMANY'S invasion of Poland and the onset of World War II, virtually all of continental western Europe lay under the control of the Nazis and their fascist confederates in Italy. Denmark and Norway fell to the Germans in April 1940; in early May, so did the Netherlands, Belgium, and Luxembourg, and most of France succumbed in the first three days of June. Hitler's armies had been thoroughly prepared for the series of "lightning strike" invasions, and countries like Denmark had been able to offer only the most token kind of opposition.

In Denmark's particular circumstance, in fact, the Nazis rewarded the Danes for their passivity by promising them a measure of autonomy. There had been no German casualties during the few moments of fighting—Denmark's King Christian X had surrendered his country's nine hundred years of independence less than three hours after German troops had waded ashore—and therefore the Germans pledged their willingness to allow the Danish government to remain in place. Courts, police, even the small army continued under Danish jurisdiction. Hitler would allow the Danes to maintain remarkable levels of self-rule, but only so long as agricultural and industrial products steadily streamed south to Germany, so long as a disruptive resistance movement did not begin to burgeon, and, equally important, so long as Denmark's "Jewish problem" did not fester.

But "there *is* no Jewish problem in Denmark," national police chief Thune Jacobsen informed Heinrich Himmler, head of Nazi police forces during Himmler's visit to Denmark soon after the occupation. Jacobsen's blunt response reflected the fact that the country's Jewish population was very small. It comprised only about eight thousand people, roughly two thousand of whom were noncitizen refugees who had escaped persecution, in Russia and Germany in particular, in the years leading up to the war. But it was reflective too of the truth that the Danes simply did not share the Nazis' maniacal conviction that the Jews whom they lived among were demons. They were *Danes* foremost, and that too was the way in which most Danish Jews perceived themselves.

Nazi officials in Berlin naively presumed that patriotic Danish citizens would feel no small measure of comfort and satisfaction under the protection of the forces that so obviously soon would win the war, and for a time, life did go on in Denmark remarkably as it had before the invasion for both Jews and non-Jews alike. Synagogues and religious schools remained open, the activities of Jewish organizations continued without disturbance, and most Danish Jews—like their Christian neighbors—found it virtually impossible to believe the rumors filtering north about the Nazi persecution, deportation, and execution of Jews elsewhere in occupied Europe. Yet the Danes never did grow comfortable with the affront posed by German soldiers and German weaponry clogging their hitherto tranquil streets. News about the true horror of the Nazi regime at last began to have a sickening ring of truth about it; and, inevitably, a vigorous Danish resistance movement did develop in time, relations between the governments in Berlin and Copenhagen dramatically deteriorating as well once the war at large began to go badly for Hitler's forces. The

Soviet Red Army ultimately had repelled the Nazis' drive deep into Russia. The Germans plainly had failed in their efforts to bomb the British into submission; their offensive in North Africa had collapsed, and even in once-compliant Denmark, sabotage against German troops carried out by Danish freedom fighters became a true irritant by the summer of 1943. When the Danish government refused to institute its own form of martial law in an effort to quell the mounting resistance, German forces took command of the king's residence in Copenhagen on August 29, arrested members of parliament as well as leading Danish citizens, and declared a state of emergency. In a response that was little more than symbolic, the Danish government promptly resigned and a general strike ensued, yet the Germans at last held complete control over the country.

Without a government to appease, and now utterly uninterested in presenting a cooperative image to the Danish people themselves, the Nazis no longer were forced to sanction what they deemed the preferential treatment of Denmark's Jews. Immediately following the introduction of the state of emergency, they confiscated lists containing the names and addresses of members of the nation's Jewish community, and soon it was terrifyingly apparent that Denmark no longer was the small but safe haven it had been since well before the onset of the war. Rumors now swirled throughout Copenhagen that a German ship recently docked in the city's harbor was waiting, impatiently, for a cargo of captive Jews.

———

THE CAVERNOUS DANISH NATIONAL ARCHIVES contain no evidence indicating that a German emigrant named Sophie Hiller or either of her two sons, Edgar or Erwin, were admitted to Denmark between 1934 and 1943. Neither do the archives contain a record establishing that Sophie's stepson Felix Hiller was one of the thousands of German refugees who had passed through Danish immigration prior to the outbreak of the war. It is possible, of course, that one—or even all—of them were admitted under false identities. Hundreds of refugees present in Denmark in 1943 entered the country by clandestine means and without official sanction, and therefore no record of their presence has ever existed.

What is irrefutable, however, is that the lives of this single family steeped in music had been ruptured in a way that would have been utterly unimaginable as recently as 1934, the year in which Paul Hiller passed away. The available evidence makes it appear certain that none of the Hillers remained in Cologne in 1943, and the reappearance of the locket likewise makes it possible that at least one of them escaped to Denmark before the late summer of that year, when the Nazis seized martial control of their occupied country and set about the scurrilous business of deporting Jews. But would Sophie, Edgar, or Erwin Hiller have been readily identifiable as Jewish in a country where that designation was deemed insignificant in comparison with the grave importance it had borne in neighboring Germany? Once in Denmark, would the Hillers have shunned their Jewish ethnicity as a further means of self-protection? Or conversely, might they have sought out that country's small community of Jews as a way to draw vital assistance and support from others who similarly were hunted? Might a member of the Hiller family have been among the large crowd that had gathered at the venerable Copenhagen Synagogue on the morning of September 30, 1943, to hear Rabbi Marcus Melchior's stunning announcement:

Last night I received word that tomorrow the Germans plan to raid Jewish homes throughout Copenhagen to arrest all the Danish Jews for shipment to concentration camps. They know that tomorrow is Rosh Hashanah and our families will be home. The situation is very serious. We must take action immediately. You must leave the synagogue now and contact all relatives, friends, and neighbors you know are Jewish and tell them what I have told you. You must tell them pass the word on to everyone they know is Jewish. You must also speak to all your Christian friends and tell them to warn the Jews. You must do this immediately, within the next few minutes, so that two or three hours from now everyone will know what is happening. By nightfall tonight, we must all be in hiding.

This extraordinary information had come to the rabbi from C. B. Henriques, a supreme court barrister and longtime leader of the Jewish community, who had received it from social democratic party chief Hans Hedtoft, who, in turn, had been personally warned by German shipping attaché Georg

Duckwitz that a Nazi *aktion* was imminent. Duckwitz first had risked arrest for treason on September 8 when he had attempted to intercept a telegram cabled to Berlin by his close friend Werner Best, the Nazis' plenipotentiary in Denmark, in which Best had recommended to Hitler that now was the right time to deal decisively with the nation's Jews. Duckwitz had failed in that endeavor, but when, ten days later, Hitler had ordered the abductions and deportations to commence on October 1, Duckwitz had been unable to stay silent. It had been solely his decision of conscience that had given members of the Jewish community the single day's notice, during which time they had been able to hide or to flee, his decision alone that had mobilized the resistance movement and thousands of hitherto passive Danes. Before nightfall on September 30, a determined, if impromptu, nationwide effort to rescue Denmark's Jews was under way.

Messengers immediately were mobilized in Copenhagen and smaller cities and towns to spread the critical word, volunteers knocking on every door they came to because theretofore there had been no general awareness in Denmark of who was Jewish and who was not. Lutheran ministers made urgent telephone pleas to their parishioners to shelter Jews however they could; resistance leaders began to marshal the aid of merchant fishermen whose boats could begin to ferry Jews to safety; Boy Scouts and members of hunting clubs combed woodlands in search of refugees who had sought the limited cover of trees, attempting to direct them to harbor towns where boats might await them; everywhere hospitals suddenly were filled to overflowing with patients whose names were listed as Hansen, Petersen, or Jensen, and as word reached the hospitals about families who were precariously hidden—or not hidden at all—ambulances quickly were dispatched to fetch them.

Taxis that otherwise would have been plying Copenhagen's cobbled streets on an early autumn afternoon now sped through the quiet countryside en route to the fishing villages that ringed the Øresund coast; and seaside trains, too, were packed as though the summer holiday season suddenly had recommenced, their hushed, grim-visaged passengers wearing as many clothes as they could fit beneath their heavy coats. Fishing ports like Rungsted, Humelbæk, Helsingør, Hornbæk, and Gilleleje began to swell with their new arrivals, townspeople opening their shops, their barns, attics, and living rooms to guests who had been utterly unexpected the day before.

Perhaps because it was farthest from Copenhagen and the perceived threat of the Gestapo, but also certainly because the train dead-ended there, the village of Gilleleje on the northern tip of Sjælland soon felt a particular surge of temporary inhabitants. On Tuesday, October 5—five days after the rescue effort had hastened to life—the evening train into Gilleleje carried 314 people instead of the three dozen it normally did, the Gilleleje stationmaster penciling the word "Jews" beside the number he scribbled in an effort to explain the flood of passengers. But these were not the first refugees to reach the town of seventeen hundred inhabitants; many had arrived in the preceding days and already had boarded fishing boats docked in Gilleleje's small harbor and safely crossed to the port of Höganäs in neutral Sweden, a dozen nautical miles across the wind-chopped expanse where the narrow Øresund met the open waters of the Kattegat Sea.

The first eight refugees—two families from Copenhagen who had not needed to wait for Rabbi Melchior's urgent announcement to sense that flight from the Nazis was about to become their only option—had escaped across the sound in the early morning hours of Wednesday, September 29. Hidden by shopkeeper Tage Jacobsen and his wife, then ferried to Sweden by retired fisherman Niels Clausen, who had lost a leg and had not been to sea for several years, but who had agreed to transport them nonetheless, the four adults and four children had been interrogated by police in Höganäs on their arrival, then quartered in a boardinghouse.

By Friday, October 1, dozens more refugees had arrived in the village. The Gilleleje Inn had been filled, as had the Badehotel, despite the fact that its owners, townspeople said, were open about their pro-Nazi sentiments. So many people who plainly hailed from somewhere else had begun to walk the streets that nervous residents began to invite the strangers into their homes, and grocer Gilbert Lassen opened the summer houses for which he acted as caretaker to refugees as well, certain that their owners would approve of his largesse. Before long, frightened Jews anxious to flee Denmark, their names almost never mentioned to their hosts, had been sheltered virtually everywhere in and around the village—in garages and lofts, in sheds and warehouses, at the hospital, the boatbuilder's yard, the waterworks, and the brewery.

Fishing cutters and oceangoing schooners from the large Gilleleje fleet had sailed unpredictably but often during the first days of the rescue. The passengers they took on board paid what they could for the short voyage to safety, the fisherman accepting payment simply because it had been irresistible not to demand it, but also because they had risked their boats, their livelihoods, even prison if they had been apprehended by the feared Gestapo. Knots of huddled refugees had waited at the docks for hours in open daylight in the beginning, then simply had walked on board a readied boat. But before long their swelling numbers, as well as the sheer numbers of embarkations, had necessitated that runs largely be attempted late at night. The ships made the crossing without the benefit of lights, and soon thereafter departures from the harbor gave way to safer and more surreptitious launches from the beaches that lay east and west of town, a half dozen refugees at a time loaded into dinghies in the seconds between the crash of each successive wave, then ferried out to the *Maagen*, the *Tyborøn*, the *Haabet*, the *Fri*, or the *Wasa* waiting in deep water.

Instead of setting a course due east to Höganäs, captains of the erstwhile fishing vessels had tended to sail north into the Kattegat as they departed the Danish coast, and only had steered eastward across the sound once they reached open water, where the likelihood of encountering German patrol boats had been even slimmer than it otherwise was. And once the trickle of refugees had reached a steady flow, the neutral Swedes—openly favoring the Allied powers now that Nazi military fortunes had begun to ebb dramatically—had done what they could to make the fishermen's round-trip journeys simpler. Swedish naval vessels made rendezvous with the Danish ships a mile or two out from the welcoming coast, their human cargo transferred on narrow gangplanks from one wave-pitched ship to another before being delivered to the Swedish harbor.

But then on the morning of Wednesday, October 6, Gestapo chief Hans Juhl, based in the nearby port of Helsingør and sniffing trouble, declared all the harbors of north Sjælland off limits to anyone who did not possess a valid fisherman's card; he instructed members of the Danish civilian coast guard to monitor carefully all activity along the shore—although the guard's allegiance to him was tenuous at best—and Juhl and his men began to make periodic raids on harbors and suspected hiding places in hopes of catching the Danes in what they perceived as blatant acts of sabotage—the secreting of hunted Jews out of Germany's grasp.

WEDNESDAY MORNING DAWNED DREARY AND over-cast, a light rain continuing from the storm that had raged in the night, and a hard southeast wind still swept across the village's thatched and tiled roofs, then out into a troubled sea. The more than three hundred refugees who had arrived by train the night before—together with those already in town but who had not yet found their way to Sweden—were dry and momentarily safe, at least, if not entirely comfortable in makeshift lodgings throughout Gilleleje and its surroundings. By the estimate of a group of townspeople meeting at first light at Oluf Olsen's butcher shop, as many as five hundred Jews whose lives were in real peril were hidden at the moment. So many refugees had descended on Gilleleje that new locations in which they could hide were becoming distressingly scarce, and the local leaders spoke urgently about how best to deal with an increasingly grave situation. Should the refugees be moved far inland somehow? Should someone try to get word to resistance organizers in Copenhagen that Gilleleje already was packed to overflowing with people who could not sail to Sweden because the Gestapo had grown determined at last to stop them? Should the townspeople attempt to organize a single, large, but inherently very risky transport, boarding most— or even all—of the refugees onto one of the large ships that had sought shelter in the harbor during the long storm? Would the captain of one of those ships agree to the dramatic plan?

Grocer Gilbert Lassen attended the meeting at Olsen's shop; so did fishmonger Juhl Jensen, high school teachers Assenchenfeldt Frederiksen and Mogens Schmidt, Pastor Kjeldgaard Jensen, and Christian Petersen, chairman of the parish council. At least six out-of-towners also were present: a man named Nielsen who sold insurance in nearby Hillerød; Niels Thorsen and Jean Fischer, resistance activists and students at Copenhagen's Technical University; Arne Kleven, a star football player a few years before, now a union administrator, and writer for the underground newspaper *Nordisk Front*; as well as Henry Skjær, the renowned, forty-four-year-old baritone from the Royal Danish Opera. Neither the well-known Kleven nor Skjær were Jewish, and therefore their lives were not in danger, but they, like the students, had become very active in organizing the escape during the preceding week, and both had arrived in Gilleleje on the packed Tuesday evening train, together with hundreds of people in flight for whom they now had assumed more than tacit responsibility.

At the close of the early morning meeting, the ad hoc rescue committee agreed that although the effort would entail serious risk, the option that made most sense was to arrange a large-scale transport and to do so as soon as possible. The students were charged with collecting money from the refugees to pay for their passage, and the teacher Schmidt volunteered to go to the harbor to convince the captain of at least one of the storm-sheltered ships that the bounty he would receive for a two-hour detour to Sweden would be well worth the short-term risk to his ship and crew. Although twenty vessels had anchored in the small harbor during the night storm, the only skipper whom Schmidt could find in the harbor area was Gunnar Flyvbjerg, captain of a large, family-owned schooner named the *Flyvbjerg*. But for the seductive fee of 50,000 Danish kroners, the captain and his mates readily agreed that they would make a single run to Höganäs, departing at one o'clock that afternoon. The hold of the *Flyvbjerg* was empty, and although its passengers could not be comfortably accommodated en route, many hundreds of refugees—perhaps even everyone in town who was desperate to go—could come aboard.

News of the impending transport spread immediately throughout the village, and in only an hour a worrisome number of refugees had begun to gather openly along the docks at the harbor, anxious about how many people the schooner could carry, and eager to assure themselves of passage. The organizers had planned to escort people to the waiting ship only in small groups, but the rush of refugees to the harbor by late morning meant that scheme had to be abandoned before it even began. Instead, hundreds of people simply swarmed the harbor area by midday—men, women, and children of all ages bundled in heavy clothing, their faces etched with fear and uncertainty, many attempting to manage suitcases, trunks, and baby carriages. Townspeople gathered too, if for no other reason than that *nothing* like this ever had occurred in Gilleleje, and everyone—whether bound for Sweden or simply there to see the refugees on their way—knew that Gestapo chief Juhl and his men might arrive from Helsingør at any moment, trapping the Jews at the water's edge before they could board and be gone.

At last people were allowed to begin making their way along a narrow breakwater to the place where the *Flyvbjerg* was moored, then to begin boarding. The crowd surged toward the stone jetty that would lead them out to the ship; people struggled to maintain their places in line; and although some were safely on board after a time, the process was terribly slow. To the dismay of many, a fisherman began to try to direct the crowd, and when someone shouted, "Throw him in the harbor! He's an agent!," others misunderstood and began to scream, "The Gestapo! The Gestapo are coming." In the seconds of panic that ensued the rumor soon seemed true, and even the *Flyvbjerg*'s captain quickly was convinced that the Nazis were bearing down on his ship. He started his schooner's motors, pushed away the desperate people who still struggled to board, then cast off, passing beyond the encircling breakwaters in only a moment and heading out to sea, stranding hundreds on the jetty, hundreds more still on shore.

Although 182 refugees ultimately reached Sweden aboard the *Flyvbjerg* that day, perhaps 300 more did not. Despite the fact that the Gestapo had captured no one, the transport plan had failed. For the moment, at least, the hundreds of terrified, perplexed, and angry people—a few separated from family members who now were en route to Höganäs—were ushered inside the big repair shed that stood at the foot of the jetty, and a frenzied meeting soon was under way to try to determine what to do next. No one had been captured, but it now seemed clear that future embarkations as large as the one just attempted, whether disrupted by Nazis or not, surely would pose similar logistical problems. A carefully crafted strategy for getting small groups efficiently onto ships had to be devised, but in the meantime, the Jews simply had to be shrouded from sight.

A small group of refugees briefly had been held at the village church during the morning while they had waited to board the *Flyvbjerg*, and it seemed to make sense to hide a larger group there once again. In an empty loft above the nave, perhaps a hundred people could be concealed—for a long time, if necessity demanded—and before the meeting broke up, Arne Kleven, the union administrator and writer, agreed to escort a group of refugees to the church and lock himself inside with them in order to assure them that they would not be forgotten. It was a promise that was to become all too easy for him to keep.

———

DURING THE SUNDAY MORNING SERVICE three days before, Pastor Kjeldgaard Jensen had read to his parishioners the letter that had been issued by the bishops of the Danish Lutheran church in response to the crisis. It was the duty of church members, the letter instructed, to protest against the persecution of Denmark's Jews because Jesus had been a Jew, because persecution was contrary to his command to love one's neighbors, and also simply because persecution "is contrary to the conception of justice that prevails in the Danish people." Pastor Jensen himself had taken the letter very much to heart: he had joined the efforts of the ad hoc organizing committee; he had made the church and the parish hall readily available for the hiding of refugees; and then, late in the afternoon on Wednesday, October 6, he went to the church door, loudly spoke the word *håbet*, "hope," the password that proved he was a friend, then was let inside by Arne Kleven. He climbed the steep and narrow stairs to the loft, then announced to the many people gathered there that as vicar of the sacred place where they now waited, he would protect each one of them with his life if called upon to do so.

The spirits of the people now sheltered in the loft had been crushed when the chaotic scene in the harbor stranded them on shore, the *Flyvbjerg*, some of their friends, even family members, embarking for Sweden without them. Many of them had spent all the money they possessed to secure passage on the *Flyvbjerg*, and despite assurances from townspeople that they would not be asked to pay again, they could not be entirely certain that that would be the case. They had been told as well that they would remain in the cold, dark, and airless loft only until townspeople could plan a way for them safely to board the *Jan*, another of the several schooners that had sought safety in the Gilleleje harbor the previous night, and whose captain also had agreed to transport refugees. This time, the plan was for the *Jan* to leave the harbor, then weigh anchor well offshore; small groups of refugees would be ferried out to the ship in dinghies in the dead of night from Smidstrup Strand, a secluded beach east of town. Kleven told the refugees that they would be transported that night, if possible. The organizers apologized for their discomfort, but they assured the huddled and desperate Jews—as Pastor Jensen had done—that they diligently would protect them until they were safely on Swedish soil.

In addition to the sixty or so anonymous people who had made their way to the loft from the harbor under Arne Kleven's escort, another group of nameless refugees who had just arrived in the village now sought the shelter of the church as the dreary day gave way to night. Before leaving Copenhagen earlier in the afternoon and traveling in taxis and private cars to Gilleleje, Henry Skjær, the opera singer, somehow had gotten word to a group of fleeing Jews about the planned transport aboard the *Jan*, and had told them that they should seek shelter at the church until the secret operation was under way. Earlier, Marta Fremming, a nurse and wife of Dr. Kay Fremming, one of the town's two physicians, had come to the parish hall—a block away from the church—to inform Grete Frederiksen, who lived in an apartment on the premises, that this new group—numbering as many as sixty people themselves—would arrive about dark, and so they did, in single carloads, beginning at 6 P.M.

Although no record survives directly linking Marta Fremming to Henry Skjær, it seems virtually certain that they must have worked jointly to bring the new group of refugees to the town and to the church. What is sure is that the unmarried Miss Frederiksen welcomed the new arrivals to the parish hall when they knocked on her kitchen door and spoke the password "hope." She made the first two dozen people as comfortable as they could be in the parish hall itself, where they spent the evening in its dark and unheated central room; the others she escorted to the church loft, where they brought the total number of people now hidden there to perhaps ten dozen.

Virtually everyone in town, of course, knew that the church was filled with Jewish refugees. Throughout the afternoon and evening, people brought blankets and coats, tureens of soup, even a roast. But as soon as night descended, it became impossible for those who were hidden to eat because it was simply too dangerous to turn on even a single light. Buckets were placed in a corner to serve as makeshift toilet facilities, but neither could they be located once night fell and the interior of the loft grew dark as a cave. The temperature hovered barely above freezing; people's hands and feet went numb; and the place was eerily silent—more than a hundred people packed into the small attic space, saying nothing for hours on end, not even daring to whisper, the only sound the incessant ticking of the clock in the tower, its maddening repetitions seeming to mock the refugees' precarious fate.

It is not clear when it happened, but at some point prior to midnight, Dr. Fremming was called to the church to attend to someone who was ill. He may have arrived with Red Cross workers, and perhaps he was called instead to the parish hall. Neither is it known how long he stayed or whether he still remained when a series of knocks were made on the heavy door. "Get out! The Germans are coming," those who were knocking whispered loudly, but whoever these people were, they did not utter the password, and Arne Kleven therefore did not open the door, and neither could he take credence in their warning.

At about midnight, however, the Gestapo did descend. They beat on the parish-hall door with pistols drawn; *they* spoke the password, and when Grete Frederiksen cracked the door to see who it was, a Gestapo officer shoved his boot in the opening to prevent her from slamming it shut, then a host of troopers burst into the place, readily capturing all the Jews who were hidden inside, only a few officers needed to detain the refugees there while the rest left for the church. Positioned beside the barred church door, Kleven could hear for a second time loud knocks and a shouted warning that the Germans were on their way—the admonition coming this time from Grete Frederiksen's brother and fiancé, whom she had been able to alert by escaping out the parish hall's kitchen door. But for the second time too, these men, speaking Danish, had not known the password, and so Kleven determined that he should do nothing more than search for alternative hiding places in the church, or for another exit, neither of which he could find.

Yet there *was* a tiny door concealed behind the altar, and Pastor Jensen was attempting to open it from the outside in order to alert Kleven and those in the loft of the immediate danger when a Gestapo agent positioned nearby spotted him. In hopes of gaining a bit of time, Jensen told the Gestapo that church sexton Aage Jørgensen possessed the only key to the building, and, accepting his story, he and Gestapo chief Juhl made their way to Jørgensen's house, where Jørgensen too helped stall for precious minutes by insisting that the key was a tricky one, and that perhaps he should come open the door himself, but the officers would have to wait while he dressed, he told them, and his dressing would be slow because his back was very bad.

Previously, the Gestapo had carried out its raids without the assistance of the thousands of German soldiers stationed in north Sjælland, but the barricaded church appeared to be a big enough prize that the Gestapo chief now ordered troops from a nearby garrison to provide assistance, and by about 4 A.M., the exterior of the church was flooded by light from automobiles and troop trucks, and was surrounded as well by battle-ready soldiers. The long night of despair suffered by the people in the loft now appeared to be ending in utter horror, but from downstairs Kleven did his best to assure the refugees that their fortress would hold. Because Kleven's key was pressed into the lock from the inside, the sexton—with the small and impatient Gestapo chief at his side—was unable to open the door, and still more terrifying moments passed before Juhl announced at the door that he now had no choice but to firebomb the building:

the refugees either would be forced out by the ensuing smoke, or they would burn to death, or they could spare themselves and open the door. It was their decision, he shouted.

At 5 A.M., Arne Kleven took a deep breath, steeled himself for whatever was about to follow, then opened the heavy door. People in the loft above him had begun to plead for him to do so, and he too knew that hope now was lost. "Where are they?" Juhl cried as he burst into the small church. "You can damn well find them yourselves," Kleven replied, and it was only seconds later when men armed with machine guns bounded into the loft, aimed blinding lights on the huddled, frozen figures they encountered there, then forced them out of the loft, into the night, and down the sloping street to the parish hall, where, together with the refugees who had been captured earlier, they waited eight more hours before they were loaded into canvas-topped troop trucks bound for the Horserød prison camp near Helsingør. A hundred and twenty Jews had failed in their desperate effort to reach exile in Sweden, and virtually all the townspeople of Gilleleje now ached with the belief that they horribly had let them down.

WE WILL LIKELY NEVER KNOW precisely when, or where, someone fleeing for his life or for hers gave Kay Fremming a coiled knot of Ludwig van Beethoven's hair, held safe in a wood-frame locket. The identity—and the unexplained motive—of that person long may remain a mystery as well.

Although rumors swirled around the small harbor town for

months, even years afterward that Dr. Fremming had been given something precious by one of the hunted refugees, he was a quiet and always insular man who appears never to have spoken openly about a most unusual gift he received on or about October 6, 1943. Nor did he ever affirm, on the other hand, that he had agreed to hold and guard the locket until its owner returned for it sometime hence. Yet whether the lock of hair was a profound offering of gratitude or simply some-one else's keepsake, which he agreed to hold in trust until the day when it could be reclaimed, it is sure beyond any doubt that this fragile bit of the corporeal Beethoven fell into Kay Fremming's possession sometime during those few days of de-termined heroism on Denmark's sea-buffeted shore.

Despite the absence of certainty, there are clues, at least, with which it is possible to piece together a scenario—or several of them—that bring the giving of the lock of hair into plausible focus. Marta Fremming did confirm long ago that the lock of hair was given to her husband in the midst of those most mo-mentous days in Gilleleje's history. It is certain as well that she and her husband were active in the collective effort to protect the Jews who rushed to their town in hopes that they could find a way to freedom in Sweden. And the fact seems in-escapable, more specifically, that Kay and Marta Fremming were in contact, if not careful collaboration, with opera bari-tone Henry Skjær, who had urged refugees to travel from Copenhagen to Gilleleje on the afternoon of October 6, in-structing them to go to the church to await passage to Höganäs on the *Jan*.

What is not known positively is whether Dr. Fremming and

his wife also hid refugees in their home or at their clinic some-time during the days of the rescue, although that probability seems quite high as well—the lock of hair conceivably given to the doctor by someone he had begun to get to know and whose debt to him seemed great. Other questions, too, re-main:

Why was Copenhagen resident Henry Skjær, already a lu-minary in the small and rarefied community of Danish music, so intimately involved in the rescue cause in Gilleleje, a provincial town that in those days was about three hours away from the city by train? Unlike Arne Kleven, whose union and journalism background made him a ready sort of activist, Skjær's profession and his notoriety, on their face, do not make it appear obvious that he would have been eager to be in-volved. Did he, like Kleven, travel to Gilleleje and attempt to help people he did not know simply out of a heightened per-sonal sense of moral and patriotic duty? Or was Skjær endeav-oring to assist one or a few persons in particular—colleagues, friends, family members? Although people clearly remember that Skjær was present at a hastily called meeting in the early afternoon of October 6, soon after the *Flyvbjerg*'s abrupt departure from the harbor, his whereabouts during the re-mainder of the day and the ensuing awful night are unknown. What is certain is that Henry Skjær informed people in Copenhagen—either in person or, more likely, by telephone—that the *Jan* would sail from Smidstrup Beach, and that its pas-sengers would wait at the Gilleleje Church to be taken to the ship. But did he, in fact, give that information to the person who then chose to flee to Gilleleje carrying with him or her the lock of hair?

Indeed, might that person have been thirty-five-year-old Edgar Hiller, also a professional singer, who had been employed by the Cologne opera when the record of his whereabouts was interrupted back in 1935? Were Henry Skjær and Edgar Hiller—resident in Denmark under a false name for some years perhaps—musical colleagues, even close friends? With Skjær's help, was Edgar Hiller hidden at the Fremming's house? Or did the doctor attend to him, or a family member, when he was called to the church? Did the donor somehow become aware that the doctor himself was much enamored of music and that he was an accomplished flutist as well?

These questions beg still others like them, yet they can be distilled into three elemental and enduring queries: Why did the locket's owner choose to give it up in Gilleleje? Why did Kay Fremming forever remain so silent about the circumstances of the giving? And was it Edgar Hiller, in fact, who gave away the lock of hair his grandfather had cut from a great man's corpse?

WHEN THE NAZIS' PRISONERS BEGAN to arrive a truckload at a time at the Horserød camp at midday on October 7, they were ushered into a windowless room where they were forced to continue the long wait until all 120 of them had been delivered from Gilleleje. At last a methodical interrogation began, each prisoner quizzed about his residence, job, nationality, and whether, in fact, he was a Jew. Those who were not Jewish, who were "half-Jews," and even those Jews who were married to non-Jews, were shuttled to a barracks to await transit to Copenhagen, where they would be released. Everyone else—about sixty people in total—was moved to wooden sheds, where the waiting continued until the group was transported again to Helsingør. There, together with hundreds more who had been captured in other places, the refugees from the Gilleleje Church were packed tightly into cattle cars loaded aboard a German ship for the overnight journey to the German port of Swinemünde, where the cars continued by rail for four more tortuous days to Czechoslovakia and the concentration camp the Nazis called Theresienstadt.

Arne Kleven, one of four Danes arrested for attempting to help Jews escape to Sweden, was jailed briefly in Copenhagen before a Danish judge sentenced him to thirty days' imprisonment for his crime—then pointedly explained that his papers would be placed at the bottom of a very fat stack. The sentence never was carried out. Henry Skjær, too, returned to his home in the capital city, but in Gilleleje the rescue effort was far from over. The misadventure with the *Flyvbjerg* on Wednesday afternoon and the tragedy at the church in the early hours of Thursday simply spurred the townspeople to find far better ways to hide the refugees, then to get them safely aboard the fishermen's ships.

When the effort's leaders met again on Thursday morning at auto mechanic Peter Petersen's house, they created a formal committee of ten townspeople—the "Jewish Committee," some among them called it—that henceforth carefully would control all rescue operations. The committee would secure the ships and regulate the fees that were charged for passage, assign hiding places and the specific tasks of the volunteers, and would ensure as well that the disorganization and poor communication that had plagued the previous days would not be repeated. Gilleleje's good name was at stake, as were human lives, said school inspector L. C. Jensen, who agreed to become the committee's chairman. Peter Petersen was charged with securing deals with cooperating fishermen; Gilbert Lassen would oversee the temporary quartering of refugees; E. K. Rasmussen, who made fishing nets, would organize embarkations from the nearby beaches; and Dr. Hjalmar Vilstrup, Kay Fremming's medical partner, was named treasurer, in charge of ensuring that all refugees could sail, regardless of what each one could pay. Surely Pastor Kjeldgaard Jensen would have joined the group as well, but the arrest of the Jews at the church—coupled with his failure to prevent it—had dealt him a terrible blow; he fell ill and did not rejoin the rescue effort again.

No one blamed the pastor for what had occurred at the church, yet clearly *someone* had told the Gestapo where they would find a large number of hidden Jews, and someone even had gone so far as to divulge the password. Some blamed the flirtatious daughter of the pro-Nazi owners of the Badehotel; others contended that a Danish secretary to the Nazi commandant of the Horserød prison camp had visited the church on Wednesday afternoon, then had seemed curiously pleased with herself when the prisoners were brought to the camp on Thursday.

The church never again was used as a hiding place, and neither were refugees sheltered again in a single place in such numbers. But the committee's diligent efforts, coupled with the extraordinary support of virtually all of the town's seventeen hundred people, ultimately resulted in nothing less than stunning success. Three hours after dark on Friday evening—and forty-eight hours after it first had planned to sail for Sweden—the *Jan* pulled its anchor in the waters off Smidstrup Beach and ferried 123 Jewish refugees across the sound. Its joyfully uneventful passage and Wednesday's panicked run by the *Flyvbjerg* were the two largest single transports of refugees during the monthlong series of undetected and unimpeded departures that ensued. On the vast majority of crossings, people traveled in small numbers, yet by the time the operation drew to a close at the end of October, with virtually all of Denmark's Jews already safely in exile, the people of Gilleleje were quietly proud indeed of what they had accomplished. During that short span of time, thirteen hundred Jews whose names they never knew—Danes as well as stateless immigrants—successfully found their way to freedom via the homes and sheds and ships of the outpost harbor town, far more than from any other village on Sjælland's coast. Nationwide, a total of 7,906 people safely were escorted to Sweden's welcoming shores in the autumn of 1943; only 580 failed to escape, 464 of those shipped like stock to Theresienstadt, among them some sixty people who briefly had sought refuge in the Gilleleje Church.

It was an astounding collective effort. It was made possible by the fact that only the relatively small numbers of Gestapo agents assigned to Denmark were enlisted by German authorities to try to stop it. Neither would the rescue have succeeded without Georg Duckwitz's valiant early warning, nor, he would contend after the war ended, without the tacit complicity of Reich commander Werner Best, who always had found a ready argument against employing army troops in the hunt despite loud demands to do so from Berlin. Yet most of all, Jews escaped in Denmark in such overwhelming numbers because Denmark's citizens agreed suddenly and en masse that they *would* escape, that they warranted persecution no more than anyone else, that the Nazi horror simply could not be countenanced in their beloved homeland.

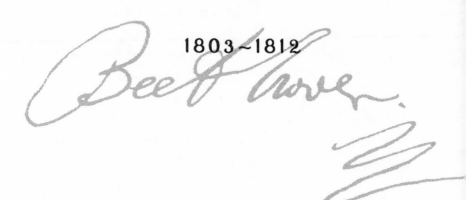

1803~1812

It was Beethoven's Third Symphony, drafted and completed in only four months during the summer and early fall of 1803, that at last clearly separated his style from those of Haydn and Mozart. He had intended to create a work that would address the transcendent subject of heroism—the triumph over pain, turmoil, and the reality of death—and as he wrote it he had become increasingly convinced that the work should be titled "Bonaparte" to honor Napoleon's heroic, ongoing effort to shape a liberated and utterly new kind of Europe. But when, in 1804, Beethoven heard the news from his friend and piano pupil Ferdinand Ries that the general had declared himself emperor of France, he flew into a rage and tore the title page of his autograph score in half. "So he too is nothing more than an ordinary man," Beethoven responded to Ries in disgust. Then he added with impressive prescience: "Now he will trample on all human rights and indulge only his own ambition. He will place himself above everyone and become a tyrant."

Retitled *Sinfonia Eroica*, the grand symphony at last was performed in public in February 1805, yet it was too lengthy, too innovative, even simply too *big* to receive initially the kind of public acclaim Beethoven had hoped for. "This long composition, extremely difficult of performance, is in reality a tremendously expanded, daring, and wild fantasia," declared the *Allgemeine Musikalishce Zeitung*. When Beethoven himself conducted the symphony at Vienna's Theater-an-der-Wien two months later, a correspondent for Berlin's arts and letters journal *Freymüthige* divided the audience's reactions into three distinct camps: those who were sure it was a masterpiece perhaps a thousand years ahead of its time; a second faction who "denied that the work has any artistic value and professed to see in it an untamed striving for singularity"; and a third, very small group, whose opinion lay in the large middle ground between the other two.

For his part, Beethoven was able to shed rather quickly his disappointments, and occasionally his revulsion, over the decidedly mixed reactions to the Third Symphony—as well as to the rest of his groundbreaking work. *He* understood the merits of his music, even if few others could join him in its appreciation, and it suited his temperament far better simply to rail against his critics and move on than to flood himself with self-doubts. Too, he had become financially successful enough by now that even his lifestyle regularly reminded him of his talents; he could afford good wine, servants, handsome lodgings in Vienna, and summer sojourns in the country. People recognized him and greeted him warmly when they passed him in the streets, and even those whose own circumstances made it unlikely that they ever would hear the performance of a Beethoven symphony or one of his signature piano sonatas nonetheless treated him with a deference reserved for someone substantial, someone who made miraculous music, a man who, in short, was a genius.

But if things were going well at the moment for Herr Beethoven, despite his ongoing physical concerns, this decidedly was not an equally good time for his adopted country. The French had declared war on the Hapsburg dynasty back in 1792, and their constant aggression and periodic attacks by now had brought the far-flung and disintegrating Holy Roman Empire close to the end of its millennial history. The rule of Emperor Franz II, who was nervous indeed about whether a French-inspired revolt of the masses soon was in store for Austria and Hungary as well, had become increasingly repressive of the common people in recent years, and even Vienna's aristocrats—otherwise occupied with lavish parties, theater, opera, and instrumental music—had to suffer distress and a bit of disruption when Napoleon's forces briefly occupied the city in 1805, then returned to bomb it into submission four years hence.

Napoleon occupied the emperor's Schönbrunn Palace and

his military commanders filled a few of the Theater-an-der-Wien's otherwise empty seats when Beethoven's opera *Fidelio* had its untimely premiere on November 20, 1805. In gestation for two years, the nascent opera had been beset by delays of several sorts, then, just prior to its long-scheduled opening, the state theater censor had declared its subject unfit for public consumption. Its libretto was the story of a sixteenth-century political prisoner in Spain who is rescued by his wife, disguised as a man, from death at the hands of a tyrannical prison governor, the kind of story that had understandably intrinsic appeal for a man in Beethoven's circumstances. It wasn't until the last moment—and the arrival of a written assurance to the censor from Court Secretary Josef Sonnleithner that the emperor's wife, in point of fact, was enchanted by the tale—that the production had been allowed to proceed. But on opening night, Napoleon's military men labeled the production nothing more than a crashing bore and the few others in attendance found it simply much too long and cumbersome. Many of Beethoven's greatest admirers, like his early patron Prince Karl Lichnowsky, who had championed the production along the way and who likely would have enjoyed it enormously, recently had fled the city out of uncertainty about whether they would be specific targets of Napoleon's wrath.

Fidelio closed after only three performances. It was revived, however—once Beethoven very reluctantly agreed to cut its length to two acts from three and reshape it—for two performances in the spring of 1806, at a time when his benefactors and ardent admirers had returned to the city. This time they were enthusiastic, but now the composer was not, and following an angry confrontation with the director of the theater, Beethoven refused to sanction future performances. It wasn't until 1814, and following still more substantial revision, that what proved to be his only completed opera—one whose trials, he contended, ought to have earned him a martyr's crown—was again presented to the public, this time at Vienna's Kärntnertor Theater, and at last to great acclaim.

From the moment of his resolute return from isolation in the village of Heiligenstadt in the autumn of 1802—determined, as he had affirmed to his friend Wegeler, to refuse to let his advancing deafness "bend or crush me completely"—until the auspicious occasion of his long-anticipated meeting with the towering German poet and playwright Johann Wolfgang von Goethe a decade later, Beethoven had composed a stunning array of music, much of which, in fact, seemed well on its way to surviving the thousand years prophesied by those who believed they heard something immortal in that original performance of the *Eroica*. Despite the fact that conversation had become much more difficult as the years progressed, and although harsh noises still attacked him as though they were knives plunged into his ears, he continued to be able to hear, at least minimally and with effort, the breadth of the work he composed in that period: five symphonies, including the spirited, sunlit Fourth; the dramatic, magnetic, and fateful Fifth; as well as the Sixth, Beethoven's Pastoral Symphony, a glorious summation of his lifelong love of nature, as well as seven piano sonatas, two violin sonatas, five piano trios, five string quartets, five concertos, an oratorio, a mass, and much more, including the overture and inci-

dental orchestral music that were written for an 1810 production of Goethe's tragedy *Egmont*.

Beethoven had been a great admirer of the plays and poems
of Goethe since his adolescent days in Bonn, and like most of
his contemporaries, he considered Goethe and Goethe's friend
and colleague Johann Christoph von Schiller to be the foremost men of letters in the German-speaking world. And
Goethe, in turn, suspected that Beethoven was led by "the
light of genius that illumines his mind like a stroke of lightning" in ways that other men simply were not, despite the fact
that the composer's work often was simply too "new" for
Goethe's classical tastes. At his suggestion—one to which
Beethoven eagerly agreed—the two men finally met in the
Bohemian spa of Teplitz while on holiday in the summer of
1812, seeing each other repeatedly during the course of a
week. But it was strangely characteristic of the mercurial
Beethoven that he took offense when his new friend responded to a piano piece he played for him simply by wiping
away tears rather than applauding. "From you, Goethe, I
won't stand for this," Beethoven loudly remanded the poet,
explaining that in Berlin in 1796 an audience similarly "had
been so educated and refined that they now staggered towards
me with their handkerchiefs wet with emotion [which] was all
quite irrelevant to a crude enthusiast like myself. . . . You
yourself must know how pleasant it is to be applauded by hands
that one respects. If you don't recognize me and consider me
as your equal, who will? To what sort of a pack of ragamuffins
shall I turn for understanding?"

Goethe had been intrigued yet substantially confused by

Beethoven's music for some time, and now that he had made the composer's acquaintance, he was equally fascinated by his personal artistry. "A more self-contained, energetic, sincere artist I never saw," he wrote to his wife from Teplitz. But then there was the *other* side of him, Goethe explained in a subsequent letter, this one sent to his friend Carl Friedrich Zelter in Berlin. Not only had the composer berated him bizarrely for failing to applaud in the way he considered proper, but he was coarse, rough, uncouth. He seemed to care nothing about tact or discretion and even less about his personal appearance, letting his hair stand out in every direction and wearing ill-fitting and soiled clothes. "His talent amazed me," Goethe explained. "Unfortunately he is an utterly untamed personality who is not altogether in the wrong in holding the world to be detestable, but surely does not make it any the more enjoyable either for himself or others by his attitude. He is easily excused, on the other hand, and much to be pitied, as his hearing is leaving him, which perhaps mars the musical part of his nature less than the social."

BEETHOVEN OFTEN HAD BEEN QUIET, even brooding and melancholy, in the years before his ears began to betray him. But his increasingly severe inability to hear the words that were spoken to him and his ever more laconic responses nonetheless did not make it impossible for him to forge romantic—if often curiously imbalanced—relationships with a series of women, as well as to harbor the continual hope that one day he would marry.

Countess Giulietta Guicciardi had been the second woman in Vienna who, for a time at least, he desperately had wished would become his mate. Two years later and keen again to find love, he became close to Josephine Brunsvik Deym, a daughter of Hungarian aristocrat Count Anatol Brunsvik and his wife, Anna, to whom he had become acquainted some years before. Josephine and her sister Therese had been Beethoven's piano pupils in the years before Josephine married—she subsequently gave birth to four children, then was suddenly widowed in 1804. Although at first he may have intended to offer her only the condolence and support of a friend, Beethoven soon was deeply in love with Josephine, openly declaring his feelings for her in a series of letters that spanned three years, assuring her that she was his "only beloved," and composing for her the song *An die Hoffnung*, "To Hope"—the wish that at last she would acquiesce and return his affections in kind. But although Frau Deym cared for Beethoven and was tempted as well by his entreaties, it appears unlikely that she ever agreed to an intimacy that was closer than a warm and devoted friendship. She, like Countess Guicciardi, would have had to ignore his modest social standing in order to allow their relationship to deepen, and marriage to Beethoven would have stripped her of her nobility and her estate. It seems sure as well that his total commitment to his music, his all-too-predictable mood swings, his eccentric personal habits and want of social graces, to say nothing of his suspect health and hearing loss, combined to convince her in

1807 that a union with him would not be best for her, her children, or indeed perhaps for him.

Yet he continued to hope that one day he would find the kind of idyllic domestic contentment that he openly had yearned for over the years, and again glimpsed that possibility in his relationship with Therese Malfatti, a niece of the Italian physician Giovanni Malfatti, who had become Beethoven's doctor following the death of Johann Schmidt the year before. Although the surviving letters between the forty-year-old composer and the young woman who was half his age do not demonstrate the kind of passionate love he expressed to Josephine Deym a few years before, Beethoven did discuss with friends his hopes to be married soon. He went so far as to write to Franz Wegeler in Bonn, asking him to search the archives for his baptismal certificate, which he would need in order to obtain a marriage license, but the relationship cooled, then ended, before the certificate was needed.

He probably never proposed marriage again, although Beethoven did continue to be drawn to sensitive, artistic women, and if they somehow were unobtainable, so much the better, it seemed. While vacationing at Teplitz in the summers of 1811 and 1812, he developed a lively and flirtatious relationship with a young opera singer named Amalie Sebald, but she lived in distant Berlin and they spent only those two summers in relative proximity to each other. And at roughly the same time at home in Vienna he had become close to a married woman, Antonie Brentano, the wife of a Frankfurt businessman named Franz Brentano, Beethoven's friend Bettina Brentano's half brother.

In 1809, while her husband remained in Frankfurt, Antonie had returned with her children to Vienna, her hometown, to attend to her aging father. She had been seriously ill for a period in 1811 and Beethoven had empathized with her physical distress, visiting her regularly and spending long hours at her piano comforting her with his music. It seems certain that Antonie encountered much in Beethoven that was missing in her domestic life in Frankfurt and that he relished her company in turn. It may, in fact, have been Antonie to whom Beethoven wrote from Teplitz in early July 1812, addressing her—or someone—as his "immortal beloved" in a passionate three-part letter that opened with his ardent determination to find a way to live with her, yet which closed in substantial doubt: "Your love makes me at once that happiest and unhappiest of men—at my age I need a steady, quiet life—can that be so in our connection? . . . Oh, continue to love me—never misjudge the most faithful heart of your beloved."

Like the letter Beethoven had written to his brothers from Heiligenstadt a decade before in which he confessed his growing deafness, it appears that this missive also was never mailed. "I must close at once so that you may receive this letter at once," he wrote, yet it, like the 1802 letter that he wrote in Heiligenstadt, was found among his belongings in the days after his death.

HAIR FOR SALE AT SOTHEBY'S

ON THE MORNING OF MAY 5, 1945, listeners in Denmark whose radios were tuned to the BBC heard the stupendous news that German forces had surrendered. By midday, the news was being proclaimed on Danish Radio as well, and British troops were entering Copenhagen and quelling the scattered shooting by German soldiers who had yet to receive the news themselves. Within twenty-four hours, everyone in Denmark, it seemed, had rushed to the capital city to observe members of the Danish Brigade, Denmark's own army, parading down the pedestrian Strøget in the city center—Danes once more in control of their sea-encircled country.

Unlike Germany, occupied Denmark had been spared the destruction by Allied bombing that had brought about the end of the war; the lives of almost all its citizens—Jews and non-Jews alike—miraculously had been spared; and its people now were giddy with delight that the long siege was over. Among their last organized acts, young Danish resistance fighters insisted, then ensured with openly brandished weapons, that defeated German soldiers made their way to the border without delay, and soon the Danish Jews who had been in exile since October 1943 began to return to their homeland. This time they simply crossed the Øresund on regularly scheduled ferries in the bright and open light of day, and for almost all of them, the welcome they received from their countrymen was nearly as extraordinary as the assistance they had been offered back when they made their secret escapes. In Copenhagen and throughout the nation, the refugees came home to find their houses and apartments secure and clean—even freshly painted in some cases—their pets and gardens well cared for, their kitchens filled with food, their jobs and their businesses eagerly awaiting their return.

Although, in time, many of the people who had fled to Sweden did go back to Gilleleje and the other fishing villages, for the time being, memories of the terror of that flight remained too raw for most to be eager to return. Yet three families—their names still unrecorded, even in nascent peacetime—did revisit Gilleleje in the days soon after the liberation to claim the three children whom, in desperate moments, they had been forced to leave behind a year and a half before: "Mona," who had been only three months old when she was taken in by Margrethe Hansen; "Henning," who had been seven months old when Edith Bæk Carlsen began to care for him; and one-year-old "Tove," adopted by Svend Andreasen's family. Each was now walking, even talking when parents they didn't recognize came to town to take them home, their tearful departures that May unambiguous proof to the people of little Gilleleje that the war had come to a close.

But it wasn't long before other children, still more victims of the ravages of the war that had devastated most of Europe, arrived in the village, reminders that its legacy would last a very long time. Early in 1946, a group of thirty French war orphans arrived in Denmark under the auspices of the Danish Red Cross, and were matched with adoptive families in several North Sjælland towns, and among the group of five who were sent to Gilleleje was a six-year-old girl from the village of Sannois, near Paris. Tiny, malnourished, but bright-eyed and fiercely independent, Michele de Rybel had been sorely in need of assistance, but she was not, in fact, an orphan. Her Belgian-born father, Theophile, was a bicycle-shop clerk and a deteriorating alcoholic; her mother Marianne struggled to feed and care for seven more children in addition to Michele, yet it was only she who was failing dangerously, only she whom her parents very reluctantly had agreed to send away.

Michele had been both confused and frightened about what was in store for her during the eight days in the spring of that year that she spent in quarantine near Sannois with as many as sixty other children, and she still had not been sure where she was going when she was put aboard a train in Paris bound for Copenhagen, carrying only a single small suitcase containing remnants of the life she was leaving behind. She was delighted to discover that the town that was her destination lay beside a beautiful sea, but the people in Gilleleje spoke a language that sounded like nothing she ever had heard, and the worst part of this new home, she soon was certain, was the family to which she had been assigned. By now it had become clear to young Michele that her natural parents intended for her to be away from France for a very long time; her mother had told her how much she loved her, but she also wanted her to live and thrive in distant Denmark. The county administrator and his wife who explained to her that they now were her parents, however, seemed strange and aloof, even cruel. They kept whole rooms of their house locked so she could not enter them; she never was allowed to play with the dolls that belonged to her new sister or to touch anything else that captured her curiosity; and often, when the rest of the family would go out, Michele was made to stay behind, locked inside the house as though it were a prison.

After three months in her new home, Michele had grown and was physically healthier, yet she was bitterly homesick and hated the circumstances of her new life. She knew that she could not manage to find her way back to France by herself, but perhaps she *could* find other people in Gilleleje who would treat her as if she truly were theirs. Not everyone in town was mean, she had come to understand. The doctor and his wife the nurse, for example, had been very kind to her when she had visited their clinic for examinations; and when Michele discovered, three months after her arrival, that they had no children of their own, she simply sat down one day in front of the large, yellow-brick house that overlooked Vesterbrogade and waited for their return, announcing to Kay and Marta Fremming when at last they encountered her that it was *their* daughter whom she would like to be.

NOT UNLIKE MANY DANES OF his generation, Kay Alexander Fremming kept much that mattered inside him—unspoken, unshared, undisclosed. No one among the people still living in the seaside town of Gilleleje who remembers the blond, blue-eyed, and friendly-countenanced physician claims to have been his confidant or even to have known him well; no one remembers ever hearing him speak at length on any topic. And although some remain sure of the rumors they heard in the autumn of 1943 that the doctor had been given something precious by one of the anonymous refugees who passed through their town en route to freedom, it appears that Kay Fremming himself never mentioned the gift he had been given—or the venerated object he had agreed to hold in trust—to anyone other than his wife, Marta, during the subsequent decade during which the couple continued to live and work in their yellow-brick house at 27 Vesterbrogade, four blocks from the small harbor where a fleet of fishing boats continued to put to sea.

Born in Copenhagen in June 1905 to parents who were teachers, Kay and his brother Kurt, three years his junior, both had had early dreams of becoming doctors. Yet while Kurt had planned to specialize—and in time did, in fact, become a psychiatrist—it was general medicine to which Kay had been drawn when he completed medical school in 1932. For the first four years of his career, he had served on staff at the Community Hospital in the city of Århus in Jylland, then, soon after his 1936 marriage to Marta Maria Rasmussen—a nurse whom he had met at the hospital, herself a Copenhagen native—the couple had moved back to Sjælland and the harbor town of Gilleleje, where until their arrival, Dr. Hjalmar Vilstrup had been somewhat dramatically overworked as the community's sole physician.

The Fremmings' new life in Gilleleje soon had proved to be the kind they had hoped for—one shaped by hard but valued work in a community where people knew and cared about their neighbors. Gilleleje was a pretty seaside town swelling with tourists and city folk in the splendid summertime, a place where the summer sun lit the sky till almost midnight. In winter, the town would shrink to a tiny knot of residents who kept indoors and out of the gales, the rain, and the snow except when it was time to take to their ships. The Fremmings and their neighbors had passed those long winter evenings at home by reading newspapers sent from the city and books borrowed from the local library, listening to music on Danish Radio as well as on cherished phonographs, a few—like Kay with his flute and Marta her cello—even making music themselves.

Early on, while the big house on Vesterbrogade was being built, the Fremmings had rented an apartment and fashioned a clinic out of the second-floor space above a clothing shop. But after that first year in Gilleleje, both home and clinic had been quartered together—the clinic downstairs this time, the private rooms above it—and it had seemed to Kay and Marta in the autumn of 1943, six years after their arrival, that this surely would be their home for a very long time to come. They had no children yet—townspeople, in fact, had begun to whisper that probably they could not—but their medical practice had consumed all of the time that they didn't otherwise reserve for a few friends and for their music. Marta, too, had joined the Red Cross as a community volunteer in the early years of the war, and it may have been because of that role that she and her husband first became active in the impromptu but impassioned effort to assist Jews in their flight from the Nazis. Yet it also may have been specifically because the two of them belonged to the small but close-knit clan of the nation's medical practitioners that their help first was sought.

Within hours after German naval attaché Georg Duckwitz first had confided that a Nazi *aktion* against Denmark's Jews was imminent, it had been doctors, nurses, and other medical professionals who had assumed key roles in the mobilization. In Copenhagen—where most of the people lived who now were in immediate danger—doctors throughout the city had been able to contact their Jewish patients and get word to them that they should consider any hospital or private clinic a safe haven of sorts. Hospital wards throughout the city quickly had been transformed into hostels, ambulances had been pressed into service as makeshift public transport, and in two dozen fishing communities along the coast, it often had been to clinics and hospitals that frightened refugees were delivered to wait again until their ships could sail.

Although the evidence is sketchy, it nonetheless appears certain that the Fremmings too had become part of this ad hoc medical network, receiving refugees into their clinic over a span of days in early October, into the living quarters that lay above it, and, for a time at least, hiding them in their third-story attic. Marta, too, had been actively involved in helping people in flight reach the Gilleleje Church on the early evening of October 6, and her husband had visited the church to attend to someone who was ill sometime before the early hours of the following morning. But apart from those few certainties—and the physical evidence of a simple black locket with a coil of hair inside—it is likely that little more ever will be discovered about how the doctor came to possess a corporeal bit of the incomparable Ludwig van Beethoven, the remarkable circumstances of that gift-giving shrouded forever by Kay's personal insularity, his kindly diffidence, and his evident understanding that neither his nor anyone else's role in rendering help to the refugees had been unique during those days and certainly should not have been labeled heroic.

THE SIXTY PEOPLE WHO HAD been taken from the high loft of the church—one of them the locket's benefactor, perhaps, each of them a "full Jew" for whom the maniacal Nazis held utter contempt—had been transported in mid-October, together with four hundred others apprehended elsewhere throughout the country, to Theresienstadt, the Nazis' way-station concentration camp in occupied Czechoslovakia, not far from the German border. There they had joined as many as 80,000 other prisoners from throughout western Europe, most of whom soon would be transferred again to the complex of death camps located near the town of Auschwitz in southern Poland, only to be replaced by nearly equal numbers of new arrivals. But because of quick and then constant political pressure directed at Gestapo head Heinrich Himmler by Danish officials in Copenhagen—as well as the curious encouragement of Denmark's Nazi plenipotentiary Werner Best—none of the Danes had ever been forced to make that final trip from which no one would return.

Danish prisoners, in fact, had been allowed to receive letters and occasional parcels of food and clothing sent from home, and on June 23, 1944, seven months after their arrival, a delegation comprising members of the Danish Red Cross and the Danish foreign ministry had arrived to inspect the camp and seek visual proof that the prisoners' basic needs were being met. Yet life in Theresienstadt—even for these "privileged" Danes—had remained brutal at best. The defeated, dignity-stripped prisoners had been fed nothing but gray gruel and an occasional bit of bread for months on end; daily they had had to perform backbreaking work despite their dramatically weakened conditions; and perhaps worst of all, a prisoners' "Elder Council" had been forced to select which captives, in groups five to ten thousand strong, would be shipped to Auschwitz each week, the prisoners themselves made to muscle their fellow Jews into the cattle cars that would carry them to their deaths.

Expressly for the nightly entertainment of the camp's guards and commanders, a group of forty prisoners who had been musicians prior to their capture had been formed into an orchestra of sorts and made to perform at six o'clock each evening as their day's physical labor at last came to a close. Each of the ten Dutch members of the ensemble had held chairs in Amsterdam's well-known Koncertgebouw before they were seized by the Nazis; three Danes had been professional musicians as well, and a fourth, fourteen-year-old Paul Rabinowitsch, a precocious young trumpet player who was accomplished enough to join the group, had been captured in the loft of the Gilleleje Church. Sometimes, people who had been professional singers and actors joined the orchestra as well and sang for the pleasure of their captors—sacred choral music, German folk tunes, and even a few songs composed by the imprisoned musicians themselves, their lyrics, like those of "The Song of Music," too subtle to enlist the Nazis' wrath:

Every day Theresienstadt has its music,
We play adagio, andante and allegro,
Cymbal and drum say bum bum ching bum ching,
Enthusiastic, the audience is applauding.
But can't you hear? There is a child crying
While the music is playing so cheerfully.

Music gives us delight and dreams
Flowing afar, outside the barbed wire,
Cymbal and drum say bum bum ching bum ching,

Enthusiastic, the audience is applauding.
But can't you hear? There is a child crying
While the music is playing so cheerfully.

And the voyagers go off. Where? You may guess,
And when they arrive at the destined place
The only thing they can bring with them
Is the music, the music, the music . . .

It had been immediately following the musicians' performance of Verdi's *Requiem* in October 1944, nearly a year after the Danish prisoners' arrival, that virtually everyone associated with the performance—the orchestra, soloists, and all of the ad hoc choir—was ordered to prepare for immediate transport to Auschwitz. Only the four players from Denmark, the boy trumpeter among them, had been allowed to stay behind; the others, it was obvious at last, had been forced to perform—to the Nazis' sadistic delight—the mass for the dead for themselves.

Six months later, on April 13, 1945, more than nineteen months after their arrival in Theresienstadt, the 418 Danish prisoners who still survived had been ordered to prepare for their departures as well. Yet they were not bound for Poland, they soon had learned, but—miraculously it seemed to them— to safety in Sweden instead. Once more, Danish leaders had succeeded in their efforts to persuade the Nazis that it made no sense to keep "permanent" prisoners at Theresienstadt, especially when Sweden would agree to take these particular prisoners off the Germans' hands.

Two mornings later, a fleet of white buses, marked with huge red crosses on their roofs and the word "DENMARK" painted boldly on their sides, had arrived at the camp and then quickly had begun to depart. For the next two days, this convoy of rescued Jews, many barely clinging to life, had had to wend its way warily through the bomb-battered cities and villages of Germany—that country less than a month away from total surrender to Allied forces—then briefly cross the island of Sjælland in Denmark before boarding boats bound for the coast of Sweden. As each bus had pulled away that April morning, the non-Danish members of a newly organized orchestra had stood nearby, playing bright marches at first, then the familiar songs, followed by a final, triumphal yet nonetheless sad farewell—the stirring melody of Beethoven's "Ode to Joy" from the Ninth Symphony offered in salute to the prisoners who were departing by others who had had no choice but to stay behind.

For the six years that Europe, and then all the world, had been at war, the spirit and the music of Ludwig van Beethoven had been claimed as their own by partisans on both sides of the terrible conflagration. For many thousands of early adherents to National Socialism, Beethoven and his music readily had seemed to prove Aryan superiority and a particular German genius in the art of music; and Adolf Hitler himself often had insisted during the 1930s that the compositions of Beethoven, Wagner, and other German masters were the noblest expressions of the Germanic soul. The performance of instrumental music had been encouraged and had thrived, in fact, during the years of the Third Reich; musicians, conductors, and composers had been assured beginning in 1939 that their artistic endeavors were key components of the war effort; German soldiers had carried pocket editions of Wagner's novella *Pilgrimage to Beethoven* with them into battle; and it had been Beethoven's Ninth Symphony—his hymn to brotherhood—that Berlin Philharmonic conductor Wilhelm Furtwängler had chosen to perform for the Führer at his fifty-third birthday celebration in Berlin on April 19, 1942.

It was the universally recognized opening motive of the great composer's Fifth Symphony, on the other hand, that had begun each clandestine broadcast of the BBC's German Service, its brief programs of music and German-language news first beamed onto the continent in 1938, then continuing throughout the war—an estimated 15 million Germans tuning in each day despite the fact that anyone caught listening to the enemy broadcasts would have been punished with death. That "fate" motive—*da, da, da, dum!*—by chance also had corresponded with the notation in Morse code, three shorts and a long, for the letter V, which had become a ubiquitous Allied symbol for victory. For millions in Western Europe's occupied nations, as well as in Britain and North America, Beethoven's extraordinary music had been wrenching evidence of the tragedy that had befallen the German people. But even in a pocket of hell like Theresienstadt, the music that once had been played in honor of the supreme architect of the madness had been, nonetheless, the same music a few of the Nazis' most desperate victims had chosen to play one day in order to herald a ray of hope.

———

IMPROBABLE AS IT SEEMS, THE proffer young Michele de Rybel made to Kay and Marta Fremming in the summer of 1946 soon was accepted. The doctor and his wife privately debated her bold proposal, then discussed it as well with her current adoptive parents, who, as it happened, admitted to being only a bit more fond of her than she was of them, and who cautioned Kay and Marta that the diminutive thing was quite a handful, in fact, before eagerly announcing that, yes, she was theirs if they wanted her. So the girl from Sannois now had yet another new home, and this time, although the fit still was less than perfect, Michele began to thrive—emotionally as well as physically. She learned Danish rather effortlessly, balked only a bit at taking music lessons, and loved exploring the town on the bicycle that soon was presented to her. It was true that she buried keys to the house out in the garden on occasion—her fear that she might be locked inside again still haunting her—but it wasn't long before Kay and Marta and their Gallic daughter Michele appeared to the townspeople of Gilleleje to be a bona fide family indeed.

Things worked out so well, in fact, that Michele's younger sister Rolande came twice with intentions to join them—staying first for the three glorious months of summer, then once again for an entire year. Eventually, however, though she professed that it was in Gilleleje where she was happiest, Rolande could not bring herself to abandon forever the family that was hers in France. For her part, Michele's sentiments always seemed the reverse; she adored the three visits to her homeland that she made while still a child, one of them in the company of Kay and Marta; the town of Sannois and the nearby splendor of Paris were wonderfully worldly in comparison with outpost Gilleleje, and she and her natural mother shared something ineffable that always was missing with often-taciturn Marta. Yet somehow, Denmark had become her home, and in Gilleleje Michele willingly remained—growing into adolescence in the big brick house in the heart of the town, playing violin now and joining her parents for impromptu chamber concerts, helping them as well in the small pharmacy at the clinic until suddenly and utterly unexpectedly, Kay's days as a Gilleleje doctor sadly were done.

It had seemed to be a minor injury in the beginning: one day in 1953 he merely had lifted his heavy medical bag and had pulled a muscle in his back, or so he thought. But the pain had grown so severe that he was nearly immobilized before long, and when he finally, and quite reluctantly, had sought medical help himself, the distressing diagnosis had been a ruptured disc that probably could be repaired only by surgery. When, in time, Kay made the decision to forgo the surgery because it bore a risk of paralysis, a second eventuality appeared ordained as well: no more could he work as a rural doctor.

For sixteen years, he had been a stalwart member of the Gilleleje community, treating the maladies and injuries and worries of nearly a thousand of his neighbors, and it had been work he loved. Never gregarious, and always presumed to be a bit apart from the crowd—if for no other reason than the way in which doctors in that era simply were presumed to belong to a separate class—Kay Fremming nonetheless had been renowned in northern Sjælland for his medical skills, his kindness, as well as for a certain sensitivity to suffering that was unusual in a man, even in one who was a physician.

But now Kay too had encountered stark, debilitating, and enduring pain, and—aware of the myriad ways in which the distress would compromise his work—he simply chose to give it up. In January 1954, Kay, Marta, and Michele—now fifteen—made the short move east to Naerum, where Kay was able to work part-time at the Øresund Hospital, then ultimately on to Holte, thirty kilometers south of Gilleleje, in May 1955, where the work that was demanded of him in the tuberculosis wing of the nearby Central Hospital in Hillerød was both manageable and rewarding in its own way.

He was only fifty years old, but the injury to his spine had forced him into the kind of life normally led by someone far older—his workday limited and etched with pain, his ability to travel and even to walk drastically diminished, his chair as a flutist in the regional orchestra and his collection of more than two hundred classical phonograph records—featuring the music of Bach, Haydn, and Beethoven—filling the bulk of his leisure time. For fourteen more years, Kay and Marta continued to live in Hillerød, during which time Michele was adopted legally at last, completed school, then married, and eventually began a family of her own. She continued to live nearby, and was in constant touch with the Danish parents whom she always had called by their given names, and Kay was delighted when he became a grandfather to her sons Carsten and Thomas. Then, on a blustery day in late September 1969, he collapsed on a train that was homeward bound from Copenhagen, where he had gone to buy new long-playing records to add to his collection. Other passengers and the conductor tried to assist him, and an ambulance was waiting at the train's next stop, but at a nearby hospital he could not be revived. Kay Fremming had died of a sudden and massive heart attack at age sixty-four.

IT WASN'T UNTIL SOMETIME DURING the first few sad and seemingly empty days after her father's death that the woman whose name now had become Michele Wassard Larsen first heard of the prized lock of Beethoven's hair that had belonged to her adoptive father. Utterly unmentioned throughout the three decades since she had joined the Fremming family, the hair and the black locket that contained it simply had lain in a drawer in the doctor's desk. Marta explained that it had been given to him by one of the Jewish refugees he had helped long ago. She could not tell her daughter the name of the person who had insisted that the doctor take it—the locket had been given to him at a dangerous time when thousands of Jews who necessarily kept their names to themselves briefly had passed through Gilleleje—but she could say without question that her husband always had valued it greatly. But why, then, had he never displayed it, and why in the world had he never shown it to her?

Kay Fremming always had been a modest man, Marta reminded her daughter. Did she ever remember him making a show of anything that he owned or had accomplished? During the nineteen months between the time when the locket came into his possession and the end of the war, it would have been foolhardy for him to have mentioned it, Marta explained. Everyone in Gilleleje necessarily kept the details of their efforts to rescue Jews quiet for fear of some sort of reprisal; Denmark, after all, still had been occupied by the Nazis, and members of the Gestapo always had prided themselves on the length of their memories. After the war, people simply had moved on with their lives, and no one who had been part of the rescue effort believed he or she had done anything that deserved celebration or special remembrance. Even once it had become safe to do so, it would have been very unlike her husband to have discussed the lock of hair or to have shown it to anyone. Doing so would have implied—at least in his mind, if perhaps in no others—that somehow he had earned the gift, that he had been heroic in a way in which others had not.

The lock of hair and the circumstances of its receipt seldom were mentioned, either by mother or daughter, following that conversation on the day in 1969 when the two of them sorted Kay's things, and for another decade, the 150-year-old locket continued to lie unmolested and rarely observed in a drawer in Marta's house in Holte. It was only in the late 1970s, on the occasion of Marta's decision to give the lock of hair to her daughter, that the peripatetic relic once more made a move of its own, this time the short distance to Michele's home in the town of Søllerød, where, for the first time in more than three decades, it saw the light of the Danish day—hanging on a wall in her living room where Michele could see it often.

———

ON A TENNIS COURT IN the town of Holte in 1964, Michele, then twenty-five, had met and immediately had been drawn to a naval officer from the West Sjælland town of Vanløse who was stationed aboard one of Denmark's two active submarines. She and Ole Wassard Larsen, also twenty-five, had married soon thereafter, and their son Carsten had been born in 1965. Their second son, Thomas, had arrived nine months before Kay Fremming's death in 1969, by which time Ole had left the navy and had accepted a position as an engineer with the Danish division of IBM. In addition to raising her sons in the town of Søllerød, Michele also had worked at a nearby pharmacy until Thomas was born—her early apprenticeship in Gilleleje still serving her well—and by 1976, Ole had become IBM's national chief of technicians, imagining that the huge multinational corporation would be his sole employer for the rest of his working life. What neither he nor his family could have known was that both his career and his life soon would be cut so short. In early December of that year, Ole had remained behind in Søllerød while Marta, Michele, and the two boys had traveled to the Canary Islands for an early-winter holiday. He had planned to join his family in a few days, but only hours after their arrival in the Canaries, Ole, just thirty-eight, had been felled by a sudden heart attack in much the same way that his father-in-law, Kay Fremming, had been seven years before. Ole had survived for almost twenty-four hours, but had died before his family had been able to reach his bedside.

Not yet forty and already widowed, Michele had struggled to support her sons by herself. She had accepted a position at the library in nearby Holte, and she and her sons had managed as best they could. By the time Marta, almost eighty-six, entered a nursing home in October 1994—her body grown weak and frail, her mind now dramatically losing its moorings, her memory entirely gone—Michele had seen the boys through school and into adulthood. And it was with her younger son, Thomas—with whom she long had shared a special bond—that Michele first began to discuss the possibility of selling the storied lock of hair.

When her mother had made inquiries late in the 1970s at the Copenhagen office of Christie's, the international auction house, she had been told that even if her dubious relic were legitimate, its value would be quite small. But Michele and Thomas began to suspect that Marta must have been given poor information. The inscription in German on the back of the locket certainly made its authenticity seem probable, and, presuming that it was indeed what it was purported to be, then surely some hairs from the head of the monumental Beethoven might be worth a great deal. Furthermore, wouldn't it make good sense for the lock of hair to be owned by someone who might revere it in ways that Michele did not? Yes, the black-framed locket with the coil of hair inside was a memento of her father, and a reminder as well of a time when he and his neighbors had refused to allow the Nazis to carry out their anti-Semitic madness in Denmark, but if Michele's mother, Marta, once knew in detail how the lock of hair specifically had factored in those events, her dementia now made it impossible for her to remember or describe them. Recently, Michele had made a gift of something else that had belonged to her father—three fragile pieces of illuminated, twelfth-century church music—to the nearby Esrum Abbey, an eight-hundred-year-old Cistercian monastery and now a regional museum; maybe there was another museum in Denmark that similarly might covet a bit of Beethoven's hair. It was soon after Michele had moved once more, this time to Hillerød, where she would be nearer her sons and her failing mother, that she and Thomas concluded that if the lock of hair actually did have real monetary value, perhaps it would be best for her to sell it. At the very least, the two of them determined to make inquiries in that regard, and so they did in April 1994.

At the Copenhagen office of Sotheby's, it was manager Anne Lehmann who first took Michele Larsen's telephone call to schedule an appointment; and it was she as well who greeted the demure and petite woman with short-cropped silver hair and her tall and striking son as they arrived at Bredgade 6 in the heart of the city on April 19. It was utterly commonplace for the office to receive queries about its potential interest in any number of reputedly rare and precious objects. Paintings by van Gogh, Renoir, even Rembrandt were presented quite regularly, in fact, although in almost every case they quickly proved to be poor forgeries. Both Lehmann and office director Hanne Wedell-Wedellsborg initially had been rather skeptical therefore about how a library employee from Hillerød might have come to possess a relic of the master composer. And how might its authenticity be determined in any case? But Michele offered them a simple and quite plausible, if nonetheless nervous, explanation of how the lock of hair had come to be hers—a Jewish refugee in flight from the Nazis had given it to her father, then a physician in Gilleleje, in October 1943, which surely was the most storied single month in the history of twentieth-century Denmark. That explanation, together with Paul Hiller's straightforward inscription on the back of the locket—as well as something ineffable about how the locket looked and felt when they held it in their hands—soon stripped the practiced skepticism from the two Sotheby's employees. The lock of hair certainly appeared as though it could be what it was purported to be, Wedell-Wedellsborg agreed, but experts at the company's offices in London would need to examine it to be sure. Would the Larsens allow her to send the locket there for inspection and a prompt response?

Within little more than a week, Michele Larsen received a telephone call from Anne Lehmann reporting the propitious news that Stephen Roe, head of Sotheby's Books and Manuscripts Department, was confident that the lock of hair in question indeed had been cut from the head of Ludwig van Beethoven, and that the company would eagerly agree to sell it on her behalf at its next "music and continental books" auction, scheduled for December. Roe had been willing to vouch for the hair's authenticity for a variety of reasons: the locket's wooden frame was consistent with those that were common in Germany early in the nineteenth century; its paper backing and inscription appeared never to have been tampered with; Ferdinand Hiller indeed had had a son named Paul who would have been thirty years old on May 1, 1883, as the note claimed; and most critically important, it was well documented in the Beethoven literature that the elder Hiller had made several visits to the dying composer in the company of his mentor

Johann Hummel, and had remained in Vienna until following Beethoven's funeral.

On May 26, 1994, Michele signed a simple contract, referencing property receipt number H151492, agreeing to allow the London house to sell at auction "1 lock of hair (framed) from Beethoven. Given as a present to Paul Hiller, whose father did the cutting of the hair 27 March 1827." The company estimated the relic's value at between two thousand and three thousand pounds sterling, and Michele in turn agreed that the lock of hair would not be sold unless a reserve price of £1,800 were met. In addition to a 10 percent commission, she would pay the cost of its transportation from Copenhagen to London, its insurance from the date of the contract until the date of the sale, as well as the cost of photographing it for inclusion in the company's forthcoming book and music catalog.

When a copy of the catalog arrived in Hillerød near the end of the summer, Michele and Thomas Wassard Larsen were impressed by the prominence with which the lock of hair had been displayed. At the top of page 22 of the impressive volume was the photograph she had funded and below it was the plainspoken description of the lock of hair:

33 BEETHOVEN (LUDWIG VAN) LOCK OF BEETHOVEN'S HAIR, with autograph note of authentication signed by Paul Hiller, son of Ferdinand Hiller, who took the cutting ("Diese Haare hat meine Vater Dr. Ferdinand v. Hiller am Tage nach Ludwig van Beethovens Tode, d.i. am 27, März 1827, von

Beethovens Leiche abgeschnitten und mir . . . übergeben. Cöln, am 1. Mai 1883. Paul Hiller"), *framed and glazed, oval, c. 10.5 x 9.5 cms.*

The fifteen-year-old Ferdinand Hiller was taken to see Beethoven by Hummel; he recorded his visits in "Aus dem Tonleben unserer Zeit" (1871: see Thayer, pp. 1044ff).

£2,000–3,000

The catalog—listing hundreds of letters, antiquarian books, and music manuscripts, but certainly no other human remains—had been mailed to book and music agents and prominent collectors around the world; the auction had been set for the saleroom at Sotheby's offices on New Bond Street in London for 10 A.M. on December 1, and now there was nothing more for the anxious seller of the lock of hair to do but wait. If it were to garner the Danish equivalent of £1,800 or more, Michele's share of those funds would be welcome and enormously helpful. If, on the other hand, no one anywhere in the world cared to pay at least that much for the relic that for so long had been harbored in north Sjælland, well, then she would be very glad to have it home again.

IN LONDON ON THE RAIN-DRIZZLED morning of December 1, 1994, agent and rare-music dealer Richard Macnutt, a virtual fixture at Sotheby's semiannual book and music auctions, paid particularly acute attention when it was lot 33's brief turn on the docket. A dapper auctioneer with a discreet gavel clasped in his palm opened the brisk bidding at £2,000, and in only a matter of moments, Macnutt—with considerable yet utterly undemonstrated satisfaction—was able to place a symbolic tick beside lot 33 in his catalog, as well as noting the price, £3,600, for which he had been able to secure the lock of Beethoven's hair for clients in the United States, whose names were not mentioned.

A letter notifying Michele Wassard Larsen of the successful sale was mailed from New Bond Street the following morning, and in two days' time a small article oddly appeared in the *Politiken,* Copenhagen's leading newspaper. "BEETHOVEN'S HAIR," it was headlined, and Michele only could assume that the paper had been tipped about the historic sale—it was a momentous one for her at any rate—by one of the two women in the Copenhagen office. "A little old lady recently walked into Sotheby's Danish offices on Bredgade," it began, and Michele was so nettled by that description of herself that she wasn't sure she wanted to continue to read. Yet perhaps a mischaracterization like that was the price you paid for a moment of fame, she recognized bemusedly, a brief renown that she—perhaps inexorably—had begun to bring on herself on the day forty-eight years before when she had sat down on the step in front of the yellow-brick house in Gilleleje in which she hoped her new parents would reside, a house inside of which a much-traveled lock of Ludwig van Beethoven's hair also, and ever so curiously, had been at home.

1813~1824

I N A L I F E L A C E D W I T H enormous accomplishment, Ludwig van Beethoven always had longed, nonetheless, for a secure and nurturing family life, the kind that as a boy he never had had. He had wanted to be married, but more than that, this gruff and awkward and often inconsiderate man had wanted to love and to be loved in return. He repeatedly had tried—and each time had failed—to become a devoted husband, then, late in 1815, he set himself on a strange and disturbing mission to become a de facto father.

In the days before his brother Caspar Carl died of consumption in November of that year, the brother had revised his will to name Beethoven as his nine-year-old son Karl's sole guardian. Yet in a later codicil altering the will, Caspar Carl named his wife Johanna as "coguardian" as well. "I by no means desire that my son be taken away from his mother," read the codicil, "but that he shall . . . always remain with his mother, to which end the guardianship of him is to be exercised by her as well as by my brother. . . . For the welfare of my child I recommend *compliance* to my wife and more *moderation* to my brother. God permit them to be harmonious for the sake of my child's welfare."

Caspar Carl had been well aware that his wife and his brother Ludwig constantly had quarreled in the years since he had married Johanna and she had borne their only child, and his anxieties about how they would share the boy's care soon proved prophetic. Within days of his brother's death, Beethoven had appealed to the Royal and Imperial Court to declare him young Karl's sole custodian, citing the fact that four years earlier Johanna had been tried and imprisoned for embezzlement. In January 1816, the court ruled in Beethoven's favor and Karl was removed from his mother's home.

Although Beethoven soon realized that he was utterly unprepared to attend to the daily needs of a child, he delighted, nonetheless, in what he had accomplished in court, crowing in a letter to Antonie Brentano—now returned to Frankfurt with her husband—that he had "fought a battle to wrest a poor unhappy child from the clutches of his unworthy mother, and I have won. He is the source of many cares, but *cares that are sweet to me.*" In the months that followed, Beethoven refused to respond to Johanna's increasingly frantic queries about her son's whereabouts and welfare, successfully convincing himself that her tarnished and unsavory reputation proved, in fact, that this "Queen of the Night" was as well as a thief, a prostitute, and that she even had poisoned her husband.

For two years, Johanna van Beethoven saw her young son only on those infrequent occasions when her brother-in-law sanctioned her brief visits—although he sometimes accused her of making clandestine trips to Karl's school, a possibility that concerned him enough that in January 1818 he brought the boy to live with him again, ordering him to keep the move secret from his mother. Twice that year, Johanna unsuccessfully petitioned the court to grant her at least limited access to her son, but when Karl ran away from Beethoven's lodgings to his mother in December, she was able to return to court again, citing his unhappiness, his poor physical condition, and his uncle's dictatorial rule as grounds for reconsideration.

In the course of making his own case to the court in December 1818, Beethoven said of Karl, in passing, "of course, if he were of noble birth . . . ," neglecting to realize as he did so that if Karl was not a nobleman, then it followed that neither was he. To Beethoven's great mortification, the case immediately was transferred to the Vienna Magistracy, the commoner's court, where this time Johanna was granted temporary custody. For another year the legal skirmish continued, with both mother and Beethoven refusing to surrender the issue until they met in the Court of Appeals a final time in April 1820. Johanna had maintained custody of Karl for another year and a half, and he professed happiness to be with her again, but this time Beethoven prevailed upon several powerful friends—including his former piano pupil, the Archduke Rudolph, son of the emperor—to do what they could to influence the thinking of the councilors of appeal. They, in turn, issued a final ruling that gave Beethoven shared guardianship of Karl, now thirteen, with his tutor, Karl Peters. Johanna lost custody of her son forever. Beethoven had paid only intermittent attention to music during much of the extended battle; his health had deteriorated dramatically—bouts of intestinal illness and respiratory infections confronting him nearly constantly now—and in the name of loving devotion he had wrested Karl from his mother for no need, and had demanded from him the kind of love that he never had been able to offer his own father.

THE YEAR BEFORE HIS BROTHER Caspar Carl's death had seen the apogee of Beethoven's popular acclaim in his adopted city. As 1814 opened, the Seventh Symphony recently had been premiered to critical delight; the Eighth had been performed for the first time in February, and with it by popular demand had been an encore performance of *Wellington's Victory*—written to commemorate the Duke of Wellington's defeat of the French the year before at the Battle of Vittoria— the splashy orchestral *pièce d'occasion* complete with jingoistic fanfares, cannonades, and even a fugal rendition of "God Save the King." In May, *Fidelio* had been revived, and when the Congress of Vienna had convened in the summer—its purpose the rather giddy redivision of Europe on the heels of Napoleon's disastrous defeat—Beethoven had composed choruses in celebration of that "glorious moment," music that was far from his finest work, but with which, nonetheless, his popularity had continued to soar.

Yet it was in 1814 as well when Beethoven had been forced to make his final public appearance as a pianist because his hearing had grown so faint. And then more trouble had descended: the postwar euphoria had been all too quickly followed by a severe economic depression, one that had left Beethoven and virtually everyone else in Vienna in seriously compromised financial conditions. The palace of his longtime patron Prince Andreas Razumovsky—the scene of a score of Beethoven's performing triumphs—had burned to the ground in December, and the count, battered by the bottomed-out economy, suddenly and almost incomprehensibly had been too poor to rebuild it. His dear friend and benefactor, Prince Karl Lichnowsky, had died that year; his brother had been claimed by consumption the next, and his stalwart patron Prince Franz Joseph Lobkowitz in turn had succumbed in 1816. In the midst of the long and onerous battle for Karl's custody, Beethoven's musical output had slowed to only a trickle; he had acknowledged as well that he was "never in good health" anymore, and during the recent weeks of protracted fever he even had begun to wonder whether he might be the next to die.

The adulation, the virtual hero-worship that had been heaped on Beethoven by Vienna's musical cognoscenti only a few years before had waned dramatically by now. The operas of Italian composer Gioacchino Rossini had become the exalted music of the moment, and Beethoven in turn spoke with deepening disdain for the place that had been his home for half his life. Vienna had grown "shabby and miserly . . . from top to bottom, everyone is a scoundrel," and few held art in high esteem anymore, he opined in great disgust. Further, and despite the use of ear trumpets, as well as a pencil he would hold in his teeth and press to his piano to help him sense its vibrations, Beethoven now was forced to compose without the vital feedback of sound. His deafness had become so complete that he could hear only what his mind imagined it had heard.

The genesis of two of Beethoven's most transcendent works also had been anchored in those ugly years of familial fighting, continuous treks to court, and enveloping silence. In June 1817, the Philharmonic Society of London had invited him, for a handsome fee, to compose two new symphonies and to travel to England for their premieres in the winter concert season of 1818. Long since repulsed by French republicanism, Beethoven now saw much to be admired in British parliamentary democracy; he felt a "particular regard and affection . . . for the English nation," and although he had no chance of meeting the London deadline and had declined to travel on account of his poor health, he nonetheless lately had begun to sketch the first of the proposed symphonies.

Closer to home, and spurred by an even more pressing completion date, Beethoven had begun work on a new mass, a nascent project in which he placed the highest importance. Eighteen years his junior, Archduke Rudolph, son of the emperor, had been Beethoven's piano and composition pupil and a real friend for many years; to him he had dedicated his Fourth and Fifth Piano Concertos, a violin sonata, the "Archduke" Trio, the *Hammerklavier* Sonata as well as the sonata that had become known as "Les Adieux," whose subject was the archduke's flight from Vienna during the French occupation. Early in 1819, Beethoven had learned that the archduke—one of the very few patrons with whom he never had seriously quarreled—was to be granted ecclesiastical honors by the church; he would be elevated to cardinal, then, on March 9, 1820, he would be installed formally as archbishop of Olmütz.

Beethoven had been neither commissioned nor encouraged to compose a mass for the occasion, but he nonetheless had set to work, neglecting to consider how great the undertaking would be or how much time he would continue to lose to litigation. Nine months later, the mass was far from finished when the archduke duly was installed as archbishop. It would be two more years before he would complete the *Missa solemnis*, more than three years in gestation, the work that by then Beethoven boldly was confident was the finest he ever had written.

IT HAD BEEN IN BONN during his adolescence, in fact, that Beethoven first had imagined setting to music Schiller's poem *An die Freude*, a hymn to the notion of a loving Father dwelling above an earthly brotherhood comprising all peoples. But nearly four decades passed before it struck him that he might conclude the monumental new symphony he had begun to sketch for the London Philharmonic Society with a chorus of voices gloriously intoning Schiller's words and sentiments. No composer ever had used voices in a traditional symphony in this way before, but Beethoven certainly wasn't deterred by the lack of precedent, and once the *Missa solemnis* was completed at long last, he set to work on the new symphony—his ninth—with a rapidity and fervor that were reminiscent of his most productive days.

It had been a decade since music-mad Vienna had hosted the premiere of a major orchestral work by Beethoven, and four years since he had made his difficult final appearance at a concert podium—conducting a charity performance of the Seventh Symphony but hearing it hardly at all. *Fidelio* had been revived for a very successful performance in 1822, but otherwise the music of the man who by now was considered something of an old master had fallen out of currency, and Beethoven had been reluctant to sanction the first performances of either the *Missa solemnis* or the new choral symphony in his home city. The depression that had rocked Vienna some years before still had not entirely abated, and Beethoven had had to struggle—and to connive a bit—with his publishers in order to continue to live in the comfortable manner he long had enjoyed. He had concocted the clever but ultimately distracting notion to sell "subscriptions"—in the form of manuscript copies—of the mass to the several crowned heads of Europe, and he simultaneously had offered its initial publication to no less than seven publishers, concealing the fact at first, then playing their offers against each other until he had been satisfied that he would be fairly paid for both the mass and the new symphony by a publisher whom he trusted, the firm Schott & Sons of Mainz.

He had made inquiries in Berlin as well about whether premiere performances of the two new works might be popular and financial successes if held there, but when news of that inquiry reached prominent members of Vienna's music community early in 1824, they responded by mailing to Beethoven an extraordinary joint appeal, signed by thirty benefactors and musicians, acknowledging in the most florid kind of language that although "Beethoven's name and creations belong to all contemporaneous humanity and every country which opens a susceptible bosom to art, it is Austria which is best entitled to claim him as her own."

The appeal moved and greatly pleased its recipient—although he was outraged when rumors briefly spread that he himself had prompted the letter's composition—and in the end he acquiesced to the scheduling of a gala concert at Vienna's Kärntnertor Theater, which would include the overture that he had composed for the dedication of the Josephstadt Theater two years before, the Kyrie, Credo, and Agnus Dei from the *Missa solemnis*, and that would be concluded by, as the announcement proclaimed, "A Grand Symphony with Solo and Chorus Voices entering in the finale on Schiller's Ode to Joy."

The response in Vienna on the heartening spring evening of May 7, 1824, was, to say the least, enthusiastic. The imperial box was empty, but otherwise the concert hall was crowded. Although Archduke Rudolph—now an archbishop in distant Olmütz—could not attend, Beethoven's longtime friends and benefactors turned out in force, among them the ailing and otherwise bedridden Baron Nikolaus Zmeskall, who was carried to his seat in a sedan chair. The renowned Ignaz Schuppanzigh was Beethoven's choice for first violin; Michael Umlauf, who had conducted *Fidelio* in 1814, commanded the podium, and Beethoven himself—resplendent in a dark green frock coat, white neckerchief and waistcoat, black silk breeches and stockings, and shoes with brass buckles, his graying hair carefully coifed and pinned for the occasion—stood nearby, setting the tempos of the several movements.

The overture and the three "grand hymns" from the mass were received with great warmth by the unusually attentive gathering, but it was the new symphony for which the audience reserved its most unrestrained responses. When timpanis thundered in the second movement, the listeners broke out into spontaneous applause, then did so four more times until at last the police commissioner yelled, "Silence!" A violent, convulsive fanfare concluded the fourth movement before a single bass voice rang out, "O Friends, no more these sounds! Let us sing more cheerful songs, more full of joy!," and then, as if in specific response to his exhortation, the entire chorus took up his theme, their collective hymn sung to joyful noise, to hope, to brotherhood: "Millions, I embrace you. This kiss is for all the world!"

When at last the voices and instruments were stilled, applause and shouted cheers erupted throughout the concert hall, but Beethoven, unnoticing, simply stood at his music stand, closing the pages of his score until the contralto soloist took him by the arm and turned him toward the proscenium so at least he could *see* the wild responses of the people whom his symphony, his song to joy, had so enthralled. His face remained expressionless as he peered out at them, but at last he offered a subtle bow—the final time he ever would stand on a stage and acknowledge the public's praise—and when he did so the applause and cries crescendoed again; white handkerchiefs waved like flags from hundreds of hands and a hundred hats rose into the lamp-lit air.

CHE GUEVARA'S HAIR

BEETHOVEN ENTHUSIAST IRA BRILLIANT NECESSAR-
ILY had focused his attention on his family and his nascent
business during his first decade in Arizona, yet his early fascination with the figure of Beethoven never had abandoned
him. The death of his only daughter eleven years before, and
his long and very slow recovery from that terrible wound, had
made him all the more astonished by what the composer had
accomplished, by what he had been able to offer to the world
despite having to contend with personal tragedies of his own.
Beethoven by now had become for Brilliant not only the vivid
personification of the might of the music itself, but also a kind

of mentor, a gruff guide through the trials of life, and increasingly he longed to possess something that the composer himself had touched—a letter, a sketch leaf, a scribbled note. By early 1975, that desire had grown great enough that now he believed he simply *had* to act, and he focused his desire on a letter Beethoven had written in 1824, one in which he had requested of Prince Ferdinand von Trautmannsdorf the use of a concert hall for the premiere of his Ninth Symphony. Beneath the text was Beethoven's large and florid and altogether beautiful signature. Yet for almost a year, the letter's $7,500 price kept Brilliant from acting. Then on December 1, 1975, he telephoned the seller a second time and was both relieved and delighted to learn that it still was available. He made a final— and rather feeble—attempt to ascertain whether the dealer would lower the price a bit, but once he had failed in that effort, his passion took control of him and he heard himself announce into the phone, "Well, then I am buying and you are selling me this Beethoven letter."

A few days later, seated with the package containing the letter on the table in front of him, Brilliant slowed to savor the moment, and as many as thirty minutes passed before he meticulously had opened the package and lifted the letter from its protective wrappings. But at last there it lay: the ancient paper was brittle and had turned a pale ocher color; the words written in German were difficult to make immediate sense of, but the broad, bold, quill-drawn signature of Ludwig van Beethoven seemed to sparkle up at him. The great man had employed that very paper 152 years before; *he* had written his name upon it, and now Ira Brilliant—who had acted impulsively in the letter's purchase, he readily would confess—at last could hold it in his hands.

It was the music of Brahms, in the beginning, to which he first had been attracted while still a teenager in Brooklyn. But it wasn't long before Brilliant's allegiance had shifted somehow, and it was Beethoven whose compositions most successfully had begun to touch a deep and important place inside him. He had loved the sonata titled "Les Adieux" in particular—the way in which it so profoundly limned the loss of someone dear—and the Archduke Trio had seemed to him to be an utterly perfect composition. He had been drawn to specific passages, to particular movements, more than he was to works in their entirety, and he had been attracted as well to the complex figure of the composer himself.

Harry Brilliant, his father (his Americanized surname derived from the Russian word for "diamond"), had immigrated to the United States from Russia in 1906 only days before he would have been drafted into the Czar's army. By the time he had married Vermont-born Anna Silverman and they had had three sons, the elder Brilliant also had established a successful business that made wiping rags out of surplus fabric. Ira, the middle son, had been groomed to supervise the technical aspects of the family business during the two years he spent at Brooklyn College, followed by two more at the Lowell Textile Institute in Massachusetts, but before he could assume that role following his father's early death, he had served in the army for three years, working during the Second World War as a chemical warfare technician in Northern Ireland and France until the Axis powers at last surrendered and he and ten million more American men had been able to come home and continue their lives.

Although his devotion to classical music never had faltered, neither had it occupied center stage for him in the early postwar years. The family business had had to be attended to, and, while vacationing in Florida in March 1947, he had met and fallen in love with fellow New Yorker Irma Maizel. The two had been married six months later, and a daughter, Maxine, had been born in September 1952. Although she had communication difficulties, she had learned to play the piano by the time she was seven—exhibiting what appeared to be an uncanny musical talent—but then she suddenly and utterly unexpectedly had died.

The pain her parents had felt in their daughter's absence, the terrible emptiness that it had seemed could never be filled, had made their once-comfortable house—and even all of western Long Island—a place from which they had been desperate to flee, and to help console his wife, Ira Brilliant had assured her that as soon as the family business could be sold and countless arrangements made, they would leave New York and journey far away.

By the summer of 1963, the sale of the business had been converted into a nest egg large enough to assure the Brilliants of their financial safety for some months. They had packed a new Pontiac station wagon with essential belongings and a few treasured possessions—including their seven-year-old son, Robert—and had struck out for a new life in Arizona. Ira had found work selling real estate—or at least attempting to—and it had been very slow going at first, but after a year of little success, he and a partner nonetheless had become convinced that the time was right to begin a business of their own, one that would focus on development in the downtown core of the small resort city of Scottsdale, just a few minutes' drive east of the Brilliants' home. A decade later, he had thrived in ways he never had imagined he might, achieving enough success, in fact, that he even had begun to consider the previously un-thinkable possibility of acquiring something that the great Beethoven had owned.

UNLIKE IRA BRILLIANT, WHO BELONGED to the gener-ation that had come of age during the Great Depression, then had spent its early adulthood embattled in war, the young man whose name had become Che Guevara a few years before be-longed to the subsequent generation of Americans, one that, beginning in the 1960s, had transformed the image of the Argentinian physician and freedom fighter of the same name into a curious kind of folk hero. *This* Che Guevara—the one now ensconced in study at the University of Texas Medical School in Galveston—never had been a true partisan of the counterculture that had emerged so infectiously during the preceding decade, yet he nonetheless took great pleasure in the nominal link between himself and the storied revolutionary.

Alfredo Guevara, Jr., had grown up in Laredo, Texas, on the U.S. side of the wide and shallow river that forms the border with Mexico. His mother's family had come from the Mexican state of Coahuila, and his father long had held a series of jobs managing gas stations in Laredo's barrios, where his young namesake had had to work as well. The boy had grown up speaking Spanish in the small, single-room block house his father had built by hand—home now to his parents and three more siblings—but once in school, he learned English rather effortlessly and soon proved to be a bright and diligent student. By the time he reached high school, "Alfredito" had read cover to cover every volume of the *World Book* encyclopedia simply because he enjoyed its breadth of subjects. As a high school senior, the science project to which he had devoted himself for three full years had earned him awards at both national and international science-fair competitions as well as the attention of Northwestern University near Chicago.

It was there in 1970 that a dorm-mate had nicknamed him "Che" Guevara on the day of his arrival, and where he first had become intrigued by classical music. He had remembered the time long before when a Laredo friend had played for him a 78 rpm recording of Beethoven's Fifth Symphony, its sounds lingering in his mind like a compelling kind of dream, but otherwise, the bronze-skinned freshman had been entirely an open book with regard to the world of music. Although he had remained a passionate Beatles fan, before long the music he most wanted to hear had been Beethoven's. His compositions, singularly and uniquely, had seemed to crawl inside the young man's chest, inside his head; Beethoven's music had seemed to be an expression of the composer's complex life experiences offered in a strictly musical language, and by the time he had returned to Texas for medical school in 1974, Che Guevara had become convinced that it was a language he wanted to listen to forever.

IF IRA BRILLIANT WERE TO continue to purchase Beethoven letters, he would need much more available capital than he currently could claim. One-of-a-kind pieces of Beethoveniana—letters, notes, sketch leafs, handwritten scores—commanded substantial prices in the mid-1970s, and only very few of them in any year were offered for sale worldwide. But the purchase of that first letter—known as "Anderson 1272" in the small and arcane sphere of Beethoven scholarship—had immediately instilled in him a desire to acquire more original material, to surround himself as best he could with vestiges of Beethoven's life and work. And, as it happened, there *was* other collectible yet affordable material to which he soon was drawn: first-edition scores of Beethoven's myriad compositions—published during his lifetime and, in almost all cases, approved by the composer himself—were comparatively much less pricey on the antiquarian music market, despite the fact that they were far from commonplace and that they often possessed significantly more musical value than the letters did. And Ira Brilliant began to imagine that if he were able to collect enough first and early editions, perhaps someday they might even form the foundation of a scholarly legacy of some kind.

His new plan for acquisitions clear, Brilliant, who remained active in real estate—his success in Scottsdale the sole means with which he could fund this new avocation, in fact—slowly began to establish relationships with the handful of European and American music dealers who traded in antiquarian music: Hermann Baron, Richard Macnutt, and Albi Rosenthal in England; Hans Schneider in Germany—as well as Mary Benjamin in Harper, New York, each of whom became well acquainted in the succeeding years with the small man whose passion for Beethoven burned so brightly. Rosenthal "would conduct business, as did all the others, with his stock surrounding him on shelf after shelf in a large room with a fireplace," Brilliant wrote in 1990. "We would visit, exchange all the news, while I would carefully ignore a small pile of music stacked on a nearby table. After a proper interval, he would casually invite me to look over the pile and make my selections. These had been saved for me."

By 1983, Ira Brilliant had assembled a collection of more than seventy first editions of Beethoven compositions—each piece possessing significant market value, the collection as a whole worth far more than the sum of its parts—and he was certain that the time had come to put the collection to work, rather than simply let it fill a closet shelf in his house. But when he and his wife Irma approached the dean of Fine Arts and the director of the School of Music at Arizona State University in nearby Tempe, they quickly were rebuffed: that institution simply was not interested. As fate would dictate a few weeks later, however, the Brilliants traveled to San Jose, California, on the heels of a convention of The Manuscript Society in San Francisco to visit David Shapiro, a friend and former economics professor at Arizona State, and currently on faculty at San Jose State University. Shapiro asked his houseguests if he might broach the subject of a similar gift to an appropriate dean at the school where he now was employed. Ira Brilliant agreed, and within days dramatically changed his life.

It was Memorial Day, May 30, 1983, when Shapiro telephoned at home Arlene Okerlund, dean of the School of Humanities and the Arts at SJSU, and quickly intrigued her enough that she proposed a meeting with him and the Brilliants at nine the following morning. At the close of that first meeting, Okerlund was nearly giddy with excitement about the possibility of building a bona fide Beethoven research center around the Brilliant collection, and before that week was out, she and university librarian Barbara Jeskalian flew to Phoenix to inspect the collection. In less than another fortnight, Ira Brilliant received a letter whose impact closely rivaled his receipt of "Anderson 1272" eight years before, yet this one was a contemporary missive drafted by the SJSU president rather than the long-deceased composer.

"On behalf of the faculty and students at San Jose State University," university president Gail Fullerton wrote, "I want to thank you for your interest in this campus as a potential home for your collection of Beethoven materials. We have an excellent music department, a commitment to developing our scholarly resources, and a love for Beethoven that is shared by the surrounding community. I do believe that working together we can achieve our shared ideal of creating *the* major center for Beethoven research in America." The letter went on to specify that if the Brilliants agreed to proceed with the project, the university would guarantee them contractually that their collection never would be sold or divided, that they would have access to it at all times, that the center would be provided with adequate, climate-controlled space in a campus library or in the music department, and that both a curator and a musicologist specializing in Beethoven would be hired to administer the center and help it meet its goal of bringing Beethoven's achievements to an ever-widening circle of students, scholars, and citizens at large.

What Fullerton proposed was the kind of publicly accessible research institution that Ira Brilliant had begun to dream about almost a decade before, and, of course, he responded quickly and enthusiastically. Negotiations between the Brilliants and the university were completed and a contract signed on September 7, 1983, creating and ensuring the existence in perpetuity of what Okerlund and Fullerton had insisted would be named the Ira F. Brilliant Center for Beethoven Studies, the only one of its kind in the Western Hemisphere. Thomas Wendel, a SJSU history professor and a keen Beethoven enthusiast himself, was named interim director; temporary space was carved out of the sixth floor of the campus's Wahlquist Library; an international search to find a permanent director got under way; and, to be sure, the still-swelling collection of Beethoven first editions—numbering seventy-seven in the fall of 1983—found its way to San Jose.

Ira Brilliant now owned a total of four important and highly coveted Beethoven letters as well, the latest of which, "Anderson 758," acquired for him by dealer Richard Macnutt, had been penned by Beethoven to Franz Brentano, husband of the woman whom many scholars believed was his secret "Immortal Beloved," and whose son Karl Josef possibly could have been sired by Beethoven. If Antonie Brentano indeed was both the composer's lover and the mother of his child, the letter's generous expression of Beethoven's hope that her husband would live very long as the head of his large and very fine family made it a remarkable document indeed. Brilliant had acquired the letter—now the crown jewel in his whole collection—only a month before he signed the contract creating the center, and soon he would amend his will to ensure that it and the other Beethoven letters also would become the property of the center upon his death. But until then, he chose to keep them in a bank vault near his home in Phoenix simply because he continued to take so much pleasure in casting his eyes on them two or three times a year, as well as exhibiting them to awestruck friends on occasion. Although each letter was protected by an acid-free mylar cover, still it was a unique kind of gift that he loved to give to a few people who could perceive its transcendent significance—the opportunity for them to hold in their own hands something that the great Beethoven had held as well.

CHE GUEVARA HAD BEEN BUOYED by the music of Beethoven during the four years he spent in medical school in Galveston, Texas, as well as the six taxing years of surgery and urology residencies that followed at the University of Arizona. Late in 1981 he met and soon married an elementary school teacher named Renée Baffert, who lived sixty miles south of Tucson in her hometown of Nogales, where a high steel fence cut across the sere hills of the small city, separating the United States from Mexico. The young doctor determined that Nogales, in fact, would be the perfect place for him to establish a practice; the area needed a urologist, particularly one who was as adept at speaking Spanish as he was at ease with English, and in 1983 Alfredo Guevara, Jr., began to earn his own income again for the first time since he had abandoned his father's gas station fourteen years before.

It took some time to build the kind of practice he long had hoped to, and although his life was enriched in the 1980s by the birth of three children, he still was a substantial distance from becoming the affluent physician he had begun to dream about being back when he was five years old and almost always hungry. But slowly, he did begin to prosper, and by 1989, he had a fine clinic with his name on the door and a bit of money in the bank at long last, and Che Guevara decided that the new space was a perfect one in which he could host a birthday party in the great Beethoven's honor. He sent out invitations to colleagues in Nogales's medical community and to friends and family members far and near. He arranged to serve an elaborate Mexican buffet and for musical entertainment to be provided by beautifully costumed mariachis; a bright banner that ringed the waiting room read HAPPY BIRTHDAY, LUDWIG VAN BEETHOVEN, and the party was such a huge success—it was the social event of the year, people contended—that the celebration became an annual event. Each year the invitation list grew larger—as did its substantial cost, of course—and in late

November 1993, Che Guevara telephoned an invitation to that year's celebration to Arizona State University professor Wayne Senner, whose article on the critical reception of Beethoven's compositions during his lifetime Guevara had read in an ASU publication. Senner was both flattered and intrigued by the generous gesture, but he informed the Nogales physician that if his goal were to invite Arizona's foremost Beethoven enthusiast—one who could rival or even better Guevara himself—then surely the name of Ira Brilliant should be added to his guest list. Che Guevara's interest quickly was piqued, and he assured Senner that he would be delighted to invite both men and their wives as well. They all would be his guests; he would house them at a nearby resort hotel, and would look forward eagerly to meeting them on the evening of December 16, when together they enthusiastically would celebrate the birth of the man who mattered so very much to them all.

IRA BRILLIANT WAS MORE THAN a little relieved to discover that Beethoven was not part of the mariachis' musical repertoire when he and his wife, Irma, traveled to Nogales in mid-December. Yet the celebration was one he greatly enjoyed being part of, and he was utterly charmed by Che Guevara. The two men discovered at the birthday party, and then in subsequent encounters, that although they were very different people, they understood each other entirely when it came to their enduring devotion to Beethoven and his music.

As the two men became more closely acquainted over the ensuing months, as they began to consider themselves true friends, Che Guevara found himself increasingly intrigued by Brilliant's collecting avocation. He became fascinated by what he learned about the tiny but intensely focused sphere of collectors around the world; he was attracted, too, by the way in which there seemed to be a kind of sacramental connection between collectible objects and the great people to whom they had belonged; he was lured as well by the financial aspects of the enterprise, which transformed attempts to buy at bargain prices and the anxious bidding at auctions into something of a heady but anxious sport. But he was captivated, most of all, by the way in which Brilliant had been able truly to bring Beethoven to life again—at least in his own heart—by gathering together scattered tokens and mementos from the time long ago when the master had made his music.

Yet Che Guevara did not begin to aspire to become a collector himself—there were his three children and their educations to think of, if nothing else—and he doubted whether the demands of his medical practice would allow him the time he would need to learn successfully the very subtle tricks of the trade. Collecting was a potential new passion he simply would surrender, but nonetheless, he would love to possess *something*, a trifle, a small memento of Beethoven or his times, he admitted first to himself, and then to his new friend. Ira Brilliant recently had purchased a printed invitation to Beethoven's funeral—a small card announcing the composer's death and the date, time, and location in the *Alsergasse* of the private service at the church outside of which so many thousands of Vienna's citizens would wait to pay their final respects. It was something precisely like the funeral invitation, Guevara explained, that he would love to possess one day, and Brilliant assured him that he would keep his eyes open on his friend's behalf. It might take a bit of time, and the memento might cost a couple of thousand dollars or thereabouts, but yes, he could garner something from Beethoven's time for Che Guevara to treasure forever.

IN THE DECADE SINCE IT had been established, the Center for Beethoven Studies that bore Ira Brilliant's name had made massive strides toward becoming the kind of institution that he, his wife, Irma, and those enthusiastic San Jose State administrators first had hoped it would be. In August 1985, Thomas Wendel, the history professor who had shepherded the fledgling center since its inception, had become president of its board and surrendered its daily administration to thirty-one-year-old William Meredith, who had been awarded a doctoral degree in musicology earlier that month by the University of North Carolina at Chapel Hill. The search for a permanent director had spread as far from San Jose as Western Europe, and several already renowned Beethoven scholars had applied for the position. But Meredith clearly had possessed not only the requisite Beethoven scholarship but also the youth, energy, and self-effacing geniality that the board had believed would be essential qualities in a successful director.

The date for the dedication of the center long had been

planned for September 15, and in preparation for it, Ira Brilliant had made a cash pledge of $50,000 to kick off a campaign aimed at raising an eventual $1.5 million endowment. He and his wife also had commissioned the construction of a fortepiano that would resemble very closely the kind of instrument that Beethoven himself had played and composed on as a young man. Built by instrument makers Paul and Janine Poletti of Oakdale, California, it would be smaller, quieter, and more fragile than a contemporary piano, and would have less range as well, yet its solid wood construction and sensitive action would allow it to echo the kind of tones with which the composer and his audiences would have been intimately familiar. An exact replica of a fortepiano that was built circa 1795 by Johann Dulcken in Munich, and for which Dulcken had drafted detailed plans, the instrument would be housed at the center itself, and would be a gift from the Brilliants in memory of their daughter.

The American Beethoven Society, a nonprofit organization of Beethoven enthusiasts dedicated to supporting its endeavors, had been formed not long after the center got down to daily business, and Patricia Stroh, who had degrees in both music history and library science, soon had been named curator. Supported in the ensuing years by grants and gifts from the National Endowment for the Humanities, the California State Library, and numerous private charitable trusts, the center's subsequent growth and its significant successes had been both swift and impressive. By the early winter day in December 1993 when Ira Brilliant first suggested to his new friend Che Guevara that he too should join the Beethoven Society in support of its myriad missions, the center had accumulated nearly 300 first editions of Beethoven's works, more than 1,600 early editions published during the composer's lifetime, and a library of almost 3,400 books and scholarly monographs in ten languages devoted to the composer's life and music. An annual piano competition for high school musicians of exceptional promise had been established, as had a Beethoven-in-the-Schools program, as well as frequent Beethoven festivals, cosponsored with the San Jose Symphony. And the center's semiannual *Beethoven Journal*, edited by Meredith, by now had published articles, letters, and commentaries by virtually every legendary Beethoven scholar in the world.

More than anything else, it was Ira Brilliant's communications and interactions with those individuals—scholarly luminaries like Joseph Kerman, Lewis Lockwood, and Maynard Solomon in the United States; William Kinderman in Canada; Barry Cooper and Alan Tyson in Great Britain; and Sieghard Brandenburg and Hans-Werner Küthen at the renowned and enormously influential Beethoven-Archiv in Bonn, Germany—that proved to him that his dream at last was being transformed into an unarguable kind of reality. He was a simple real estate man, after all; for many years he had been nothing more than a Beethoven layman, a mere foot soldier of sorts, yet his long-term commitment had resulted in his early seventies in burgeoning friendships with the world's foremost authorities on Beethoven's life and his work. They called him by his first name, he was proud to note, and by now he called them by theirs as well; they respected his wide-ranging store of knowledge; they recognized what an important institution the center he had established had become, and, to a person, it was clear that they were beguiled as well by Ira Brilliant's profound and particular passion.

In all his years of collecting, however, Brilliant never had been able to acquire a fine first edition of Beethoven's Opus 1, the Piano Trios numbers 1–3, which had been published in 1795, three years after the composer's move to Vienna from Bonn. Beethoven was by no means widely renowned in those early days, and only a handful of the first edition of the trios survived to the present day. Not only was a first-edition score rare, but its opus number lent it a particular cachet, and Brilliant and the center's staff were eager to find a copy and acquire it, if its cost were not too dear. And it was in early November 1994 that good fortune seemed to arrive once more in the mail. In the catalog for Sotheby's semiannual books and music auction, Brilliant spotted precisely what he had been looking for: lot number 27, to be sold in London on December 1, was a first-edition Opus 1 in excellent condition. Sotheby's estimate that it was worth £1,500–2,000 was a bit daunting, but Brilliant quickly determined to do what he could to secure it. He would make as generous a pledge as he could, and other key supporters of the center likely would do so as well, and together surely they could arm English agent Richard Macnutt with funds sufficient for its purchase.

But there was something else in the catalog that also quickly caught his eye. In the two decades since he had become a collector, he never had encountered human remains of any kind being offered at auction, yet there it was unmistakably: lot 33, its value estimated at £2,000–3,000 and its authenticity certified as unassailable, was a lock of the great Beethoven's hair. When he broached the possibility of purchasing the lock of hair with Meredith and Wendel, both were immediately enthusiastic, and then Brilliant remembered his friend in Nogales.

He was able to reach Che Guevara at his clinic at the close of the day, and Brilliant first reminded his friend that he had asked him to find a suitable Beethoven memento sometime. Yes, of course, the doctor remembered. In that case, and now barely concealing his excitement, the senior man posed a subsequent question: would Che by chance be interested in acquiring a bit of Ludwig van Beethoven's *hair*?

It was an extraordinary notion—a lock of the master's hair that one day he might hold in the palm of his hand, Beethoven himself alive again, or at least undeniably among the living—and Che Guevara enthusiastically affirmed that he would pledge $5,000 toward its acquisition. Brilliant thanked him both for his generosity and his quick decision, but he cautioned him that, based on Sotheby's own projections, it might take twice that amount to secure it. Yet he too could contribute, and surely there were a few other members of the Beethoven Society who might as well. He would do what he could to put together a small consortium of buyers, and they would make their best collective effort to bring to the United States this unlikely but enormously intriguing relic. Imagine it, the two men urged each other: a bit of Beethoven's *hair*.

THE FIRST ORDER OF BUSINESS was to marshal the financial resources that would be necessary to acquire both the Opus 1 score and the lock of hair. During the succeeding days, American Beethoven Society president Tom Wendel eagerly added $500 to the hair-acquisition pot, as did longtime supporter Caroline Crummey; Che Guevara had pledged $5,000, of course; Brilliant also could contribute $2,000 or so over and above the amount he had committed to Opus 1, but as he tallied the several contributions, he believed he could authorize his agent Richard Macnutt to bid no higher than £4,200. That amount *might* fetch the relic, but who knew? The item at auction would be Beethoven himself, in point of fact, so it seemed entirely possible that someone somewhere in the world might be willing to spend a princely sum to secure it. When he faxed his final instructions to Macnutt a few days before the sale, Brilliant made it clear to his agent that, should they fail in their attempt to acquire Opus 1 as lot 27 was auctioned, then he should be aggressive in his attempt to acquire two other, if decidedly lesser, Beethoven first editions that also would be auctioned. If they lost Opus 1—and he sorely hoped they would not—Macnutt then should focus his efforts on them, as well as that beguiling bit of hair held in a small black locket that was labeled lot 33.

A fax from London was waiting for Ira Brilliant when he got out of bed on the morning of December 2, 1994, and the news from Richard Macnutt was both bad and good. The Opus 1 score had sold for £6,500, more than three times the Sotheby's estimate, and almost twice what he had been authorized to bid.

On the other hand, Macnutt had been successful in acquiring the "Farewell Song" and Serenade for Flute and Fortepiano first editions, and yes, he also had purchased on Brilliant's behalf the lock of Beethoven's hair. No one had chosen to better Macnutt's high bid of £3,600 for lot 33, and although he had been prepared to go a good bit higher, of course, the gavel had fallen before he had been forced to do so—meaning that Guevara, Brilliant, and their partners would spend a total of about $7,300 once Sotheby's surcharge, Macnutt's commission, and the shipping charges were tallied. Macnutt informed his client that although the bidding on the hair had been brisk at its outset, it quickly had reached its upper limits, and, given what they might have had to pay, Macnutt wrote that he believed the winning price "was in a sense quite comfortable."

His *hair*. Ira Brilliant and his partners now actually owned a bit of Beethoven's hair. Nothing akin to it might ever be offered again, he realized before another notion nearly buckled his knees. He and Irma and Che Guevara and their cluster of associates in San Jose soon would be able to hold something of the great man himself in their quavering hands. It truly was extraordinary, but he tried to be calm as he placed an urgent call to Nogales.

"Do you have your comb ready?" he asked when he heard Che Guevara's voice.

IRMA BRILLIANT WAS MADE MORE than a little uneasy by the package that sat unopened on her husband's desk for three full days. The circumstances did not seem to her to be very different from possessing the cremated remains of a stranger, albeit one who had been held in the highest regard. Finally, however, Ira was ready to open the package; there had been a mounting kind of pleasure for him in letting it sit unattended, in knowing what treasure it contained yet keeping that treasure at bay, and then, in much the same way he had with his first Beethoven letter two decades before, he spent most of an hour meticulously unwrapping the Sotheby's packaging before at last he held the black-frame locket in his hands and saw with astonishment the hair that had grown on the head of the man whom he revered more than any other.

When Brilliant and he met in Tucson a few days hence, Che Guevara responded in kind to his first glimpse of this most unlikely prize. Neither man spoke for a moment when Brilliant removed the locket from the small box in which he had carried it from Phoenix, and their silence bespoke their shared emotions. This hair, this remarkable relic of Beethoven himself, was not something they had endeavored for years to obtain; neither man, in fact, had known of its existence just six weeks before, yet the improbable dispatch with which it had come into their possession didn't diminish in any way the profundity of that moment in which they first viewed it together.

It was at that same meeting, however, when a significant misunderstanding between them first came into focus as well. Although prior to the auction the two had discussed the fact that they would divide the hair if it became theirs, its acquisition had been uncertain enough that the particulars of the split never had been discussed. Now that the lock of hair belonged to them, however, it was time to begin to settle issues of that sort, and Guevara made it clear that it seemed to him that the division should be based on the amount each had invested. It seemed to him that since he had paid $5,000 of its $7,300 cost, two-thirds of the hair therefore belonged to him. But Brilliant was quick to disagree. As *he* saw it, Guevara had supplied the largest share of the hair's purchase price, yes, but on the other hand, it was he who first had learned of the pending sale, who had employed his English agent in its acquisition, who had paid the entire cost of the two first editions, and who would have been willing as well to spend more than the $1,300 he ultimately had contributed to the hair's purchase if he had needed to do so. Brilliant did not offer his own proposal for how the hair should be divided—what seemed equitable simply wasn't clear to him as yet—but he did say that he hoped much of the hair ultimately would be housed—in perpetuity—at the Beethoven Center in San Jose.

The two men agreed to give the matter more thought, and soon the subject of their conversation shifted. Might it make sense, Dr. Guevara wondered, to test a bit of the hair, to have it examined by forensic scientists? Was it possible that testing of the hair that lay on the table between them might be able to announce something conclusive about the last days of Beethoven's life? Could it demonstrate what medications he had consumed? Could it conceivably explain the reasons for his chronic intestinal distress, or even decipher his deafness?

This was a thrilling thing for the two men to consider: in his Heiligenstadt Testament, penned nearly two hundred years before, Beethoven himself had expressed the hope that one day the reasons for his hearing loss might be determined and made public, and now perhaps the two of them could help fulfill the composer's poignant request. Was *that* the reason why, they asked themselves, the hair so serendipitously had come to them?

UNDER USUAL CIRCUMSTANCES, IT IS Sotheby's policy not to disclose the sources of the objects it presents at auction. But on this occasion—on the appeal of Ira Brilliant and Che Guevara and, of course, because of the renown of the man whose hair the locket contained—Stephen Roe, head of Sotheby's Books and Manuscripts Department, agreed to contact the previous owner of the hair, explaining that the people who now held it hoped they might learn something of its particular and unlikely provenance. Roe made it clear when he wrote to Michele Wassard Larsen in Denmark that she was under no obligation whatsoever to surrender her anonymity or to describe how the lock of hair had come into her possession, but, as it happened, she was very willing indeed. Two months after the arrival of Beethoven's hair in America, it was followed by a letter posted from Hillerød and mailed to the Beethoven Center in San Jose. "Hello!" the typed missive called out,

My name is Thomas Wassard Larsen, and i am writing to you about a lock of Beethovens hair, sold by Sotheby's auktions i London. I hope you understand the meening with this letter, because i'm not very good at writing in english.

The lock was owned by my mother, who had to sell it due to her economical situation. My mother Michele was born in France a cupple of years before 2.nd world war. During w.w.2 my grandmother had 8 kids including my mother, and she could not feed them all so therefore my mother was adopted by a nice family in Denmark. She was now in the age of 8 years.

My mothers new parents were a Doctor and a nurse who lived in a little town in North Sealand called Gilleleje. This little town was one of the closest to Sweden, to witch many judes fleed during 2.nd w.w. Many of these judes were wery poor and some of them had som awfull deceases.

My mothers new father who was a doctor helped many of these judes, in the start only with medicin, but later he worked together with the local fishermen, in the night to smuggel judes to Sweden. It was one of these judes who gave the lock of Beethovens hair to him for his help. My grandfather kept this medallion until his dead in 1969, the same year that i was born.

Thomas Larsen wanted the locket's new owners to know how pleased he and his mother were that Beethoven's hair had gone to people who greatly appreciated it, who would honor it as they always had. And yes, he said, they would welcome continued communication and would offer whatever help they could in unraveling more of the locket's history. Thomas

Larsen knew that his grandfather had been a humanitarian, to be sure, but the young man also wished to know more about who the Jews had been and how his grandfather had helped them survive. Were they called Hiller too, their name the same as the one inscribed on the locket? They had reached safety in Sweden, he hoped, but then what had become of them?

What Thomas Larsen's letter conveyed was dumbfounding new information: it appeared that Ludwig van Beethoven—most unwittingly and far more than a century after his death—had played a small yet nonetheless significant role in helping Jews escape the German killing machine. It was news that transfixed Ira Brilliant in particular—he had fought against the Nazis and was a Jew himself—and soon after the receipt of the letter, the young Dane's queries became questions he now resolved to try to answer, solutions to these enigmas suddenly every bit as important to him as were the potential explanations of Beethoven's diseases that forensic scientists someday might deliver. Like Thomas Larsen, Brilliant and Guevara and everyone in America associated with this improbable lock of hair now hoped they could succeed in tracking the descendants of Paul Hiller and his father, Ferdinand, the man who had met the mighty Beethoven and who secreted the relic away. In the tumultuous aftermath of World War II, did members of the Hiller family travel on to England, to the United States, or to the nascent state that was taking shape in Palestine? Had they been able to repair their lives in the decades between the war and now? Had they—as the great composer had done—eventually found a way to overcome awful adversity?

IN THE MONTHS SINCE THE purchase of Beethoven's hair, Ira Brilliant, Che Guevara, and the center's staff had begun to discuss in some detail the possibility of testing the hair, and had had preliminary conversations with scientists as far away as the Massachusetts Institute of Technology and as near at hand as the Lawrence-Livermore Nuclear Laboratories, less than an hour's drive from the Beethoven Center in San Jose. But long before any analysis could begin, the issue of the hair's ownership and its division had needed to be decided, and by the early summer of 1995, Brilliant had suggested this possible resolution to Guevara: most of the hair, 73 percent of it, in fact, would become property of the Beethoven Center, where it would remain in perpetuity, and where it conceivably could be made available sometime far into the future for testing with forensic tools that did not exist in the present day. It would be labeled the "Guevara Lock of Beethoven's Hair" in acknowledgment of the physician's key role in its purchase and of his generous gift to the center. The remainder of the hair would become Che Guevara's sole possession, and he could do with it what he chose, although the center would have the first option to purchase it if it ever were offered for sale. Any contemporary testing would employ strands from this portion of the lock, and Guevara himself would be the key decision maker with regard to what tests were performed and by whom.

At Ira Brilliant's urging and in advance of his response, Guevara had traveled to San Jose that summer to visit the center for the first time as a means of gauging its mission and its merits for himself, as well as to attend the annual "Beethoven Bash" sponsored by the American Beethoven Society. While there, his impromptu cheerleading had succeeded in raising the final portion of funds needed to purchase a print of the renowned 1814 Letronne-Höfel Beethoven engraving, and Brilliant had come away from their joint visit to California hopeful that the physician ultimately would agree that San Jose was the place where most of the hair belonged. And soon thereafter, Guevara had, in fact, reached the same conclusion; he had consulted both his heart and his pillow, he informed his friend, and he would agree to Brilliant's proposed disposition of the lock of hair that henceforth would bear his name.

Several more months passed before contracts were ready to sign certifying the terms of the agreement, and before Che Guevara had succeeded in assembling a team of medical and scientific colleagues who would take the first step in a forensic process that likely would take some years to complete. But finally, on the morning of December 12, 1995, all the necessary advance work had been completed and a coterie of interested individuals were prepared to meet at the University of Arizona Medical Center for the signing of the documents and then at last to open the locket that held the precious hair—the first time its contents had been exposed since frame maker Hermann Grosshennig had refurbished the locket in Cologne precisely eighty-four years before. Dr. Guevara himself would perform a sort of surgery on the locket late in the morning. Observing and offering their separate kinds of expertise would be conservator Nancy Odegaard, Dr. George Drach, a professor of urology for whom Guevara felt great loyalty and affection, and forensic anthropologist Dr. Walter Birkby, each from the University of Arizona; forensic pathologist Dr. Richard Froede, a former Pima County medical examiner; and Ira and Irma Brilliant, of course. And there would be others watching the procedure as well: local television news teams and print reporters would attend; Amy Stevens, a *Wall Street Journal* staff reporter, also would be on hand; and a British Broadcasting Company crew would film the event as part of a documentary they were producing on Beethoven's life and music.

It was going to be a thrilling day, and Ira Brilliant had been eager to get under way before the traffic got bad early on that Tuesday. He was excited, of course, but he also felt curiously bemused as he negotiated his way through the crush of cars on Interstate 10. It was all so wildly unlikely, wasn't it? He was living a kind of dream, and it was truly hard to believe these improbable circumstances: there in the backseat of the Buick en route to Tucson was a small and inconspicuous box inside of which was Che Guevara's hair—carefully coiled strands that were, in point of fact, a miraculous bit of Ludwig van Beethoven himself.

1824~1826

BY THE MIDDLE OF THE 1820s, Beethoven required regular assistance not only with musical and financial affairs, but also with his rather more mundane domestic requisites. In the thirty-two years he had lived in and around Vienna, he had never bought a home—although he long had had the means to do so—in largest part because something in him demanded a constant change of scene, but also because he and landlords quickly tended to find causes for quarrel. With each of his more than forty moves, Beethoven had prevailed upon friends, then later friends and servants, to assist him, all of whom were well aware that the request surely would be repeated within six months or so. Although he could be shrewd in negotiating with music publishers the price he would charge for a new piece, he was notoriously poor at household computations, concluding one time after much difficult cogitation that the sum of eleven halves must total ten and a half. And once servants had become integral to his household, he even had required advice about how he ought to interact with them. "What ought one to give 2 servants to eat at dinner and supper both as to quantity and quality?" he had inquired of a friend. "What allowance per day do the housekeeper and maid receive? How about the washing? Do the housekeeper and maid get more? How much wine and beer? Does one give it to them and when? Breakfast?"

Servants had come and gone constantly during the years in which he had been able to afford their services; most he would fire within two months of their arrival, a few would vanish after only a day of the deaf man's tirades and wild demands. Nephew Karl now tried to be with his uncle as often as his university studies permitted, and when Schindler and Beethoven parted company in the wake of Beethoven's accusations about purloined receipts from the gala concert at which his Ninth Symphony was premiered, he was replaced—but still without payment—by Karl Holz, also a violinist, yet one who was rather more gifted than Schindler in that regard, and someone of whom Beethoven grew very fond during the year before Holz's marriage quite curtailed the amount of time and assistance he was able to offer. In much the same way that they always had, Beethoven's benefactors and longtime friends—who, of course, were drawn to him for the music he made, but also because something about the irascible old goat was curiously dear and even lovable—continued to visit him with regularity, always inquiring about his welfare and enjoying his good company on those days when his spirits were bright.

Good moods, however, were limited by ever more illness. When his ongoing gastrointestinal woes and yet another unremitting fever sent him to bed in the spring of 1826, Dr. Anton Braunhofer, a well-respected professor at the university, prescribed a strict diet absent coffee, wine, spirits, or spices of any kind, one that seemed far more cruel than potentially palliative to the patient who had few pleasures. But the fever slowly subsided enough that Beethoven was able to travel in May to the nearby spa town of Baden, where the doctor hoped daily mineral baths also might be efficacious. Yet Beethoven's condition did not soon improve. "We are in bad health—still very weak and belching and so forth," he reported in a letter to Braunhofer. "I think that a stronger medicine is going to be necessary, but one which is not binding. And now surely I should be allowed to drink white wine diluted with water, for that mephitic beer is simply revolting. My catarrhal condition is as follows: I still spit a good deal of blood, but only from my windpipe, I presume. Blood also frequently flows from my nose and my stomach has become dreadfully weak, and so has, generally, my whole constitution." Still capable, however, of a bit of merriment, he closed his letter with the notation of a short, sixteen-bar canon, its two lines stating, then repeating the playful phrase, "Close the door against death, Doctor; I plead that these notes will help with my need."

Despite the continual trials of illness, Beethoven's ability to make music had not yet been reduced solely to the composing of comical ditties, however. Although he had not written a string quartet since 1810, he had been intrigued three years before by Russian prince Nicolas Galitzin's offer to commission three quartets, which, by advance arrangement, would be dedicated to him. The prince had let Beethoven set his own price and the composer in turn had assured him that the first quartet could be finished quite soon, but the demands made by the *Missa solemnis* and the Ninth Symphony had, in fact, delayed the quartet's completion until February 1825. Beethoven always had found something wonderfully therapeutic in the composition of music—it was the sole medication he reliably could count on—and this time he also took particular pleasure in returning to a form he long had overlooked. While still in Baden, where daily mineral baths at last seemed to be helping him as well, he set to work on the second quartet, which he quickly completed. The quartet's *molto adagio* third movement was a "Hymn of thanksgiving to the Almighty, in the Lydian mode, offered by a convalescent," he wrote on the score, and beside its lilting, up-tempo section he scribbled "Feeling new strength."

He felt strong enough, in fact, to begin work on Galitzin's third quartet—the last one required of him—while he remained in the country, completing it in Vienna at the end of the year, yet still he was compelled to keep writing. More abdominal illness—this time accompanied by painful joints and a worrisome return of pain in his eyes—interrupted work on a *fourth* quartet in the winter, but it too was virtually complete in July 1826, when Beethoven was shattered by terrible, nearly incomprehensible news.

"My mother met him on the Glacis, completely undone," remembered Gerhard von Breuning, son of Stephan von Breuning, his early friend from Bonn, who had moved to Vienna with his family many years before. "Do you know what has happened? My Karl has shot himself!" Beethoven announced, impossibly. "It was a glancing shot; he is still living, there's hope that he can be saved—but the disgrace he has brought upon me; and I loved him so." It was emblematic of the nature of his relationship with his nephew that Beethoven considered the horrific event's effect on his reputation as readily as he worried about the boy's survival, but there was no doubt, nonetheless, that the attempted suicide devastated him. "The pain that he received from this event was indescribable," Gerhard von Breuning recalled. "He was cast down as a father who had lost his much-beloved son."

Although always eager to please him, Karl, now nineteen, increasingly had been plagued by his uncle's demands, his possessiveness, his constant suspicions and quick anger. Beethoven disliked Karl's friends and had become ceaselessly mistrustful of their motives; he complained that the boy was lazy, a spendthrift, and he had been outraged when Karl continued to see his mother surreptitiously. For his part, and prior to the incident, Karl had informed his uncle's assistant Karl Holz that he simply had grown "tired of life because [I] see in it something different from what [my uncle] judiciously and righteously would approve." "I grew worse because my uncle wanted me to be better," he explained to the police after the fact, and so on July 29 Karl had pawned his pocket watch, bought two new pistols, and traveled to Baden, where, high on a hill that for many years had been one of his uncle's favorite hiking spots, he had fired both weapons at his temples, fully intending to kill himself.

One bullet had missed Karl's head entirely, however, and the other, incredibly, had failed to penetrate his skull. He had been found, barely conscious, and had been hurried back to Vienna, where first he had been taken to his mother's house, and then to a nearby hospital. As had happened the previous summer in Baden, this time too Beethoven was assumed to be a peasant when he arrived at the hospital to see his wounded nephew. But when a physician's assistant finally acquiesced to his insistence that he was the famous composer, the shabby old man quickly took the assistant into his confidence, explaining that he "did not really want to visit [Karl] for he does not deserve it; he has given me too much vexation," then taking time to outline the boy's many misdeeds before at last he asked to be taken to his room.

It was late September before Karl was released from the hospital, by which time Beethoven finally had begun to contend with the possibility that his own behavior toward his nephew might have played a part in pushing him toward suicide. He never openly admitted as much, but he did agree that Karl now should be allowed to join the army, something he had wanted to do for some time, and Beethoven also made a last-ditch endeavor of sorts to patch his splintered family back together. Although he did not attempt a direct rapprochement with

Karl's mother, he did, in the end, acknowledge that Karl should spend a bit of time with her before he began his military service, and he even went so far as to write to Johanna, henceforth offering her Karl's half of her husband's pension and adding that "should I be in a position later on to give you a sum from my bank for the improvement of your circumstances, it will certainly be done." He had wished her "all possible good" as he concluded that letter, and now he seemed to wish the same to everyone who carried the Beethoven name, agreeing at last to his brother Johann's plea that he and Karl, who was still convalescing, should come stay for the remainder of the autumn with him at his small estate near the village of Gneixendorf.

Beethoven long had despised Johann's wife because he believed—not without evidence—that she had cuckolded her husband repeatedly, but Johann, a pharmacist, assured his brother that he would "scarcely see the woman," and a curiously wistful Beethoven not only soon became comfortable in residence with his brother, but also was captivated by the bright and open countryside that spread away from it toward the Danube and the distant Styrian mountains. "The scenes among which I am sojourning," he wrote to his music publisher in Mainz, "remind me somewhat of the Rhine country that I so greatly long to see again, having left it in my youth." As had been commonplace for some time, however, he often was withdrawn and on some days was terribly depressed. And despite the fact that he also continued to be ill with worrisome regularity, he was at ease enough at Gneixendorf now that he managed to return to work on a fifth quartet, which he had begun in July a few days before Karl's attempted suicide. Although more modest in scale than the previous quartets, there were aspects of the new piece that yet again pointed in novel directions. "What I write now bears no resemblance to what I wrote formerly. It is somewhat better," he declared, still buoyed by new challenges. He called the last movement of the quartet "The Difficult Resolution," its title unintentionally ironic, since he could not then know that it would be the last complete piece he ever would finish, his work on it done in December before a terrible row with his brother and alarming new medical troubles persuaded him that it was time to return to the city.

VERY MODERN MICROSCOPES

IT WAS AN UNUSUAL PUBLICATION in which to see his byline, and the language in which the article was written was one he didn't speak, but nonetheless they both had appeared in the September 1995 edition of *Jødisk Orientering*, the monthly newsletter of Copenhagen's "Mosaic," or Jewish, community. "Last December, a fellow Beethoven lover and I acquired a certified lock of Beethoven's hair in London," Ira Brilliant had begun, his words translated into Danish by the newsletter's editor, Birte Kont. "We learned that it had been consigned by a woman in Denmark. We were contacted by her son who told us that the lock was given to her by her father. His name was

Kay Alexander Fremming." Brilliant had gone on to tell the compelling story that Fremming's grandson first had described in a letter mailed to the United States six months before, and the American had outlined for Danish readers as well the intriguing journey the hair had made through time and the war-scarred nations of western Europe. Because it appeared that Beethoven had been involved—albeit very indirectly—in the saving of a Jewish life, and because he saw such powerful symbolism in that possibility, Brilliant had appealed to Denmark's contemporary Jews for any additional information they might have that would shed more light on the circumstances that long ago had led to the giving of the black locket to Dr. Fremming. And Brilliant had expressed another hope as well: "I am always interested in data concerning Beethoven and his influence on western culture, and as an American Jew I am also eager to help spread a story of man's concern for his fellowman, as personified by the spontaneous effort of the Danes to help their fellow Danes in their hour of need."

Ira Brilliant first had written to Birte Kont at the suggestion of New York University psychology professor Leo Goldberger, a childhood immigrant to Denmark from Germany, one who still had been a schoolboy in October 1943 when he and his family were forced to flee to Sweden from their Copenhagen home. Although Goldberger had lived in the United States for many years by now, he returned to Denmark often, and in 1987 he had edited *The Rescue of the Danish Jews*, an English-language collection of memoirs and essays by prominent Danes who had participated in those terrifying events. Goldberger himself, however, had not passed through the town of Gilleleje en route to safety, and therefore had been unable to offer specific assistance when Brilliant first had written to him. Yet he, like so many others already, had been fascinated by Thomas Wassard Larsen's story of how his grandfather had come to possess a lock of the immortal composer's hair, and the professor had suggested numerous people whom Brilliant might contact in addition to the editor of *Jødisk Orientering*. In particular, Goldberger was aware that a retired Roskilde University professor named Christian Tortzen had published in Danish some years before a book titled *Gilleleje, Oktober 1943*, which had focused solely on how the events of the rescue had unfolded there.

It had taken Brilliant some months to locate and then hear from Tortzen, but when at last he received a letter from him on the same afternoon he returned home from watching Dr. Guevara open the locket in Tucson, the news Tortzen had for him was disappointing. His book had begun as an oral history project undertaken with students late in the 1960s when he had been a high school teacher in the north Sjælland town of Hillerød, a few kilometers south of Gilleleje. He had become so fascinated, and so moved, by what the residents of the small seaport had described to him and his students about that turbulent time that he subsequently had felt honor-bound to compile their collective stories into a book. And yes, of course, he informed Ira Brilliant, he was familiar with who Dr. Fremming had been, but no, neither he nor his students had been able to interview him prior to his death in 1969, and neither had anyone ever told Tortzen a tale about a gift of a lock of hair. Nonetheless, he assured the inquiring American in his boldly scribbled hand, "I am trying to find persons who have known Dr. Kay Alexander Fremming in order to identify the Jewish refugee who gave him the hair lock. You will hear from me later."

THE OPENING OF THE LOCKET on that December day had been a wonderful event, both reverential and riveting, as moving as it also had been etched with anticipation, and its several participants had come away quite hopeful that they had set in motion the eventual discovery of important new information—whatever it might be—about Ludwig van Beethoven's long-battered health, data now hidden in strands of his graying hair. And even that very day, new findings about both the hair and its sketchy provenance had been forthcoming: the locket in which the hair had been housed was identical to those that were commonplace in early-nineteenth-century Europe; it had been refurbished in 1911, or so a bit of paper found inside attested, and that likely explained why the strands remained in surprisingly good condition. The hair appeared two hundred years old, or thereabouts, forensic anthropologist Walter Birkby had declared, and under microscopic examination, Birkby also had noted the presence of a few follicles at the roots of individual hairs, meaning that organic DNA testing likely would be possible, if it was deemed appropriate.

It wasn't until a few weeks hence, however, that Birkby startled Brilliant, Guevara, and their colleagues by informing them that his meticulous count had revealed that the presumed

150–200 hairs numbered, in fact, 582. Young Ferdinand Hiller had snipped away much more hair than anyone previously had supposed, and therefore the Beethoven Center would receive 422 individual hairs—an amount large enough that, once returned to the locket, its volume would appear hardly to have been diminished—while Dr. Guevara would claim 160 strands for himself and for the testing that soon would get under way. The larger sample, together with the locket in which it had resided since the 1820s, would be housed in a temperature- and humidity-controlled vault at the Beethoven Center in San Jose. Dr. Guevara would choose simply to curl the hairs that now were his inside a sterile petri dish, its lid held tight with a silver ribbon, which in turn he placed inside what he believed was his fireproof, bombproof, and theftproof office safe. Beethoven's hair would be nearby as he saw his patients each day, and that certainty greatly appealed to the physician, yet he also was ready to announce in March 1996 that a few of those peripatetic hairs were about to travel again.

In collaboration with members of the Tucson-based team that had observed the opening of the locket, and in regular consultation with Ira Brilliant as well, Dr. Guevara lately had designated two scientists who initially would be entrusted with the precious relic. First, he would ship twenty hairs—none of them containing a follicle or so-called "bulb"—to Dr. Werner Baumgartner, head of Psychemedics Corporation in the Los Angeles suburb of Culver City, California, who would complete a drug analysis of the hairs before forwarding them in turn to Dr. William Walsh's Health Research Institute in Naperville, Illinois, for further and far more extensive analysis.

In the months since the search for the proper scientists had commenced, Dr. Guevara, Ira Brilliant, Walter Birkby, and pathologist Richard Froede separately had been in contact with dozens of research scientists at laboratories and universities around the United States and had found them almost universally interested in taking on the unusual project. Each had been informed that the person ultimately selected would be required to agree to several key conditions: the work would be conducted according to the highest contemporary scientific standards; the name of the subject from whom the hair had come would never be attached to the sample; the testing would be completed in a timely manner and would be done free of charge; the sample would be returned immediately to Guevara on his verbal request; and all findings would be kept utterly confidential, unless Guevara were to give the scientists his express permission to publicize them. Those demands had deterred no one in the end, and ultimately the physician had based his decisions in largest part on the scientists' collegial reputations; the twenty hairs from Beethoven's head would go to Baumgartner and Walsh, the doctor explained, simply because their colleagues had affirmed that they were the very best in the business at the kinds of analyses both were eager to undertake.

SOON THE SEARCH FOR MORE information about the locket's trip through time necessarily spread from Denmark to Germany as well. With the frequent assistance of his friend

Hans-Werner Küthen at the Beethoven-Archiv in Bonn, Ira Brilliant was able to determine by the time the testing got under way that Paul Hiller—to whom the hair had belonged from May 1883 until at least December 1911 and perhaps until his death in 1934—had been an opera singer in his youth, as his mother had been. A 1922 edition of *Wer ist's? (Who's Who?)* noted, however, that he had spent the majority of his working life as a music journalist; he had married Sophie Lion in June 1902 and she had borne him two sons, Edgar in 1906, and Erwin two years later. It was curious that a 1959 edition of the *Musiklexikon* failed to mention either his wife or their sons, yet it did note that in 1882, twenty years before his marriage, Paul Hiller had fathered a son named Felix during the time he lived in the city of Chemnitz. Felix almost certainly would be deceased, Brilliant and Küthen agreed, as would Sophie Hiller; but although both men would be elderly by now, it was possible, wasn't it, that one or both of Sophie's sons remained alive? Yet where—and how—on earth could they be found?

With the dedicated assistance of a Frau Gödden (whose first name she never surrendered) at the Nordrhein-Westfälisches Hauptstaatsarchiv in Düsseldorf, Brilliant finally was able to piece together a Hiller family tree that reached back as far as Ferdinand Hiller's parents, Justus Hiller and his wife, Regine, and which reached far enough forward in time to record the names and birth dates of the grandchildren of Tony Hiller Kwast, Paul Hiller's sister and only sibling. But nothing Brilliant or his assistants in Germany could find offered new information about what had become of Paul Hiller's wife or any of his sons. It seemed probable, of course, that their lives had been disrupted dramatically by the rise of Nazism and the subsequent state-sponsored persecution of Jews that had begun early in the 1930s, but so far at least, there was no way to be sure. The 1933 *Adressbuch* for the city of Cologne declared that Paul Hiller and his son Edgar, who was listed as an opera singer by profession, resided at 31 Eifelstrasse, just off the small Eifelplatz, near the city's southern railway station. Published a few months after Paul Hiller's death, the 1934 edition of the directory listed Sophie Hiller and son Edgar as still in residence; by 1935, only Sophie Hiller still resided there, or so the directory claimed; and by 1936, *no one* from Paul Hiller's family appeared to live in Cologne any longer.

Surely Sophie Hiller or one of her two sons had fled north to Denmark at about that time, Ira Brilliant now presumed, and had taken in tow the storied lock of hair. It also seemed probable that one of the three, or conceivably all of them together, had been safe in Copenhagen or its environs until October 1943, when they had been forced to flee again. But the townspeople had known virtually none of the names of the refugees who passed through Gilleleje en route to safe haven in Sweden. And if that were the case, would it ever be possible to *prove* who had pressed the locket into Kay Fremming's hands?

"IN MY SCIENTIFIC AND PHILOSOPHIC battles, I have derived much solace and strength from Beethoven's music," Werner Baumgartner wrote in his report to Dr. Guevara and

Ira Brilliant when he completed his examination of the twenty hairs Guevara had sent to him. He wanted the men to know therefore how much the opportunity to test the hair for the presence of morphine had meant to him. Baumgartner was a native of Austria, and certainly his nationality made him feel a kind of kinship with the great composer, yet there was something more that drew him to Beethoven: Baumgartner was a long-standing disciple of the Vienna-born philosopher of science Karl Popper as well. Popper, who died in 1994 and who also had been an accomplished composer and musicologist, believed that Beethoven remained the world's foremost "subjective" composer, someone who "had made [his] music an instrument of self-expression" in a way that would have been disastrous, even "dangerous," without his "purity of heart, his dramatic powers, his unique creative gifts." In much the same way that it had seemed to Popper, Baumgartner also suspected that Beethoven never could have expressed that profound subjective emotion had fate not forced him to suffer chronic and profound physical pain, and it was in that context that the Los Angeles scientist was so startled by the finding his test produced.

Since 1977, Baumgartner and his colleagues at Psychemedics Corporation had tested more than two million human hair samples using a patented procedure capable of detecting the presence of morphine, heroin, and other opiate metabolites, and had struggled—at last successfully—to convince a legion of skeptics that examination of hair for drug use was, in fact, far more accurate than urinalysis. Baumgartner, his wife Annette, and two colleagues first had published the results of their comparison of drug testing of both hair and urine in the *Journal of Nuclear Medicine* in 1979, but more than a decade had passed before their procedure had become widely considered the state of the art. Capable of detecting drug concentrations as small as a billionth of a gram in weight, the Baumgartner method utilized radioimmunoassay, a laboratory technique first developed in the 1950s by Nobel laureate Rosalyn Yalow, which combined radioisotope tracing and basic immunology to create a very accurate and straightforward means of measuring minute concentrations of biological and pharmacological substances in blood or other fluid samples. Baumgartner's proprietary method of hair radioimmunoassay by now was employed by more than sixteen hundred police departments, parole departments, corporations, schools, and universities around the United States, and successfully had withstood numerous challenges in court. In a series of studies undertaken by the National Institute of Standards and Technologies during the 1990s, seven rounds of "blind" hair samples had been sent to laboratories across the country, and Baumgartner's had been the sole laboratory that was 100 percent successful in identifying both positive and negative samples.

What was particularly important with regard to testing the Beethoven sample was that Baumgartner and his colleagues had been able to establish some years before that trace amounts of opiates remained stable in human hair over very long periods of time. In 1986, they had examined a lock of hair that had been clipped from the head of English poet John Keats following his death in 1821, and had found that it still contained significant levels of morphine 165 years later, a finding consistent with the knowledge that Keats, also a chemist and physician, had self-prescribed laudanum, an opium tincture then widely used as an analgesic, while he was dying of tuberculosis. A subsequent Psychemedics analysis of hair from a five-hundred-year-old mummy unearthed in Peru had shown that it still contained trace amounts of cocaine, although most of the drug that was present by now had broken down into its byproduct benzoylergonine. If Beethoven had consumed opiates in the last months of his life, therefore, evidence of that fact certainly should have been revealed. But what Baumgartner found instead—or what he didn't find—seemed nothing less than arresting, and he explained how he had reached his surprising conclusion in his report to Dr. Guevara and Ira Brilliant:

The analysis began with the washing of the twenty hair specimens in dry ethanol at 37 degrees centigrade with vigorous shaking at 120 cycles/minute. The purpose of the wash procedure was to remove any possible morphine contaminants from the hair surface. Any morphine found in the ethanol solution would be interpreted as morphine deposited on the hair not as a result of drug use but by morphine that was present in the environment while Beethoven was alive or during the many years of storage of the hair sample.

After the initial decontamination process, the hairs were dried to remove any residual ethanol. The subsequent extraction was performed with specially deionized water which was received from Dr. William Walsh's laboratory. The use of the specially purified water was desirable in order to avoid introducing any metals (present as impurities in the water) into the hair specimen during the extraction process. Prior to extraction with water, the hairs were quickly rinsed with 2 ml of water to remove any remaining ethanol, which could interfere with the radioimmunoassay (RIA) procedure. The hair was subjected to 15 hours of extraction at 37 degrees centigrade with a fresh 2 ml aliquot. The ethanol wash solutions were evaporated to dryness and the residue taken up in water for RIA analysis. RIA was performed in duplicate on 0.5 ml water aliquots. The results of the analysis showed *zero* morphine content in the water extracts, in the water rinse, and in the ethanol wash solution.

Based on that finding—and assuming, of course, that the hair tested truly had been Beethoven's—Baumgartner was willing to claim without equivocation that the composer had not been treated with morphine or any other opium derivative during the last months of his life, and this newly uncovered information greatly intrigued him. "During most of his adult life, Beethoven was plagued by very painful but undiagnosed medical conditions, and his death appears to have been particularly painful," the scientist wrote. "Nevertheless, he was still creatively active on his deathbed. In my opinion, Beethoven could not have remained creatively active if he had been sedated with morphine. Not finding morphine in his hair, I believe, therefore speaks volumes about his character, particularly about his disposition towards adversities."

Those final words belonged to a long-standing Beethoven admirer rather more than an utterly objective scientist, yet they nonetheless illuminated the essential significance of Baumgartner's finding: given the contemporary quality of the medical attention the composer received during his final days, it was logical to assume that he would have been offered morphine as a sure means of mitigating his suffering, yet now it appeared that—if offered, in fact—he had refused the drug. And if he *had* declined to accept pain-relieving sedation, wasn't the sole plausible explanation for the refusal the likelihood that he preferred instead to keep his mind as clear as possible so he could continue to sketch music? In none of the written accounts by Beethoven's last two physicians, Drs. Andreas Wawruch and Giovanni Malfatti, did either man acknowledge having prescribed an opiate for the dying man. Wawruch spoke only of administering "a severe counter-treatment for inflammation," as the composer's final illness commenced, and although Malfatti later was asked to provide additional therapy, the only record that survives lists his treatment—one that briefly was efficacious, in fact—as nothing more than an iced alcoholic punch.

It is the fact that the greatly infirm composer continued until the last week of his life to sketch music for what might have become a new string quartet that surely shapes the strongest anecdotal evidence in support of Baumgartner's finding. Two decades earlier, during what had been his most productive compositional years, the man whose greatest carnal pleasure had been the consumption of champagne nonetheless seldom had allowed himself to consume more than a little on evenings when he planned to work the following day. That wondrous beverage sadly clouded his ability to concentrate, he had explained, and its aftereffects stripped him of the vital energy he required as he composed, and so he very reluctantly had refused to allow himself its regular pleasure. At the end, perhaps Beethoven simply never was offered the blessed, pain-free fog that morphine might have induced. Yet it was also possible—as the Los Angeles scientist now suggested, nearly two centuries after the fact—that Beethoven pointedly had declined it, much as he had done in earlier years when he had denied himself champagne. Perhaps the sharply focused work of sketching music, even on his deathbed, seemed to him to be the better medicine.

IT MIGHT HAVE BEEN A latter-day medicine that Dr. Kay Fremming had given to an ill refugee that in turn had elicited the gift of the lock of hair, although no one could be sure. There was very little, in fact, about the circumstances of the giving that anyone knew in 1995 or seemed likely to be able to discover, yet for Ira Brilliant it simply was unacceptable not to try. He read everything he could find about the remarkable heroism of the Danish people, their deeds becoming renowned worldwide in the decades after the war. In books by historians Leni Yahil and Harold Flender, Danish Rabbi Marcus Melchior, and in Leo Goldberger's anthology of essays, Brilliant learned how at the end of September 1943 naval attaché Georg Duckwitz had alerted Danish leaders to the impending purge; how doctors and nurses had led the way in the Danish citizens' bold and immediate response to the crisis; how frightened Jews—Danes and immigrants alike—had been escorted to fishing villages along the Øresund coast, where they had been hidden until they were put aboard boats for the brief but perilous transport to Sweden; and he discovered as well that it was in the little port of Gilleleje where, on the night of October 6, the rescue effort had gone terribly awry, someone betraying to the Gestapo the fact that as many as 120 Jews were hidden in the high loft of the Gilleleje Church.

Jens Noe, pastor of the church in 1995, had no knowledge about a lock of Beethoven's hair when Brilliant contacted him that autumn, although he promised to query the old-timers who still remembered vividly the traumatic events of another fall fifty-two years before. Danish playwright Finn Abrahamowitz, who had written a play about the events in the church, based largely on Christian Tortzen's book, could offer Brilliant no new information; neither could Per Jørgensen, administrator of Gilleleje's regional government, nor Henrik Lundbak at the Frihedsmuseet, the National Resistance Museum in Copenhagen; and no one who had read Brilliant's earlier plea for assistance in the Jewish community's newsletter ever responded with a specific memory, a promising lead, or even idle speculation about who might have given the small and venerable locket away.

Each new possibility that Ira Brilliant pursued, in fact, proved fruitless during the three years that followed, and it wasn't until Michele Wassard Larsen and her son Thomas took up the search themselves in 1998 that at last a few leads began to emerge, clues pointing to the moment when someone—filled perhaps with both fear and gratitude—had given Beethoven's hair to her father. On a blustery Sunday in October of that year, Michele and Thomas and Thomas's partner, Lena, shared coffee and pastries with retired fisherman Julius Jørgensen at his home in Gilleleje and were fascinated by what he had to tell them. He had been seventeen years old that fateful October, and his father Aage had been sexton of the church. It was his father who had stalled for time as the Gestapo demanded that he surrender the key to the church's heavy door, and it was his father too who had told him soon thereafter that Dr. Fremming had been called to the church earlier in the night to attend to a refugee who was ill. Aage Jørgensen had been quite clear about that detail, and he had told his son something else: there was a rumor, nothing more than that perhaps, that the refugee had given something "precious" to the physician in return for his help. Indeed, the rumor was alive in town in the following days, Julius Jørgensen remembered, but he cautioned his visitors that they should not make too much of what he had to tell them. The Fremmings had hidden refugees in their home as well, and the gift could have come from one of those people, or the rumor might simply have been one of those stories that somehow springs to life of its own accord, absent an anchor in truth. Yet the one thing of which he could assure them absolutely was that the doctor did visit the church loft a few hours before its inhabitants were captured.

Julius Jørgensen's memories set in motion a flurry of new contacts and nascent possibilities for the eventual resolution of the riddle. Once informed that the lock of hair might have been given away at the church, Odense University history professor Therkel Stræde—who was on sabbatical at Georgetown University in Washington, D.C., in the fall of 1998 and with whom Brilliant had been in communication—suggested that because roughly half of those who had been captured in the church loft ultimately had been deported to Czechoslovakia, it would be wise to contact members of *Theriesenstadt-Foreningen*, a survivors' association that neither Brilliant nor the Larsens theretofore had known of, to inquire whether one or more of them might be able to shed substantially more light on Dr. Fremming's visit. The organization's chairwoman, Birgit Krasnik Fischermann, had been a small girl on the night she and her family were captured, and she remembered very little about those frightful hours in the church loft, but Paul Rabinowitz—his surname now changed to Sandfort—a friend and fellow survivor and a retired music-history professor, had been sixteen at the time.

As it happened, Paul Sandfort's memoir of his family's flight from the Nazis, their capture, and eventual imprisonment in Theriesenstadt—titled *Ben: The Alien Bird* and published under the pseudonym Paul Aron—was about to be rereleased in Israel in an English-language edition, and the book made the horror of that night and the subsequent sixteen months of incarceration dramatically manifest. But Paul Sandfort—like those who had been queried before him—knew nothing about someone hidden with him and his family in the church who might have carried a lock of Beethoven's hair, then given it away in the hours before the capture. Neither could he confirm Julius Jørgensen's claim that Kay Fremming had come to the loft to offer medical assistance, yet he *did* remember a small group of visitors whom he always had presumed were Red Cross representatives. Fremming's wife, Marta, had worked for the Red Cross, in fact, and now Michele Wassard Larsen wondered whether her mother and her father had gone to the church under the protection of the bold red insignia in order to give someone specific aid, but Paul Sandfort could provide nothing more concrete than that—there had been so many people packed into the small space, he explained, and it had been so frighteningly dark.

Yes, of course, he knew who Henry Skjær had been, Paul Sandfort subsequently wrote in English in response to the questions now pressed upon him from America. Sandfort was a musicologist after all, and had sung with the renowned opera baritone in a Danish student performance following the war. "I could easily have asked him [about the lock of hair]. I was sent to Gilleleje by Dr. N. R. Blegvad, who was the doctor for the singers at the Royal Theatre, so he probably did that in collaboration with Henry Skjær, who was often a soloist with the University Choir of Copenhagen where I was a first tenor. Henry Skjær surely knew that I was in the loft, but we never talked about it. Maybe he was embarrassed of the fact that I was taken by Germans?"

Christian Tortzen's book, *Gilleleje, Oktober 1943*, plainly had described Henry Skjær's active role in the rescue effort in the seaside town. Tortzen had been told by at least one former refugee that it was Skjær who had directed her and her family to the Gilleleje Church, and—together with the news that the Royal Theatre's physician directed Jews to Gilleleje—a very tenuous kind of connection at last began to emerge between the musical milieu in which Paul Hiller's family had been at home in Cologne and the appearance of a lock of Beethoven's hair in a far distant Danish fishing village. Skjær, in fact, had been a key figure in the small world of Danish vocal music; in 1925, he had made his first appearance at the Royal Opera in Copenhagen—singing, as it happened, the role of Don Pizarro in *Fidelio*, Beethoven's renowned opera of love and freedom from imprisonment; and two years prior to that premiere, he had married Copenhagen resident Ida Levy, a Danish Jew. Tortzen explained when he was queried again that in the autumn of 1943, "Henry Skjær had a house in Snekkersten, south of Helsingør [and not far from Gilleleje]. In this house were gathered 30–40 persons in the first days of October, Ida's relatives and Jewish friends. Skjær's son was a pupil of Mogens Schmidt, who went to the house and together with Skjær planned the escape of the Jews. Skjær was in Gilleleje from Tuesday the 5th to Thursday the 7th and in the middle of the events. His wife's sister was arrested by the Gestapo, but Skjær had her freed because she was a 'half-Jew.'"

Christian Tortzen did not know whether other refugees whom Skjær had hidden subsequently had been captured, and neither could he know, of course, whether one of those people had been a German whose surname was Hiller. Yet could it simply have been an extraordinary kind of coincidence that a lock of hair that once had belonged to former opera singer

Paul Hiller in Cologne—and whose son Edgar had been an opera singer when he disappeared in 1935—was given to Kay Fremming sometime during the days in which a well-known Danish baritone was clandestinely at work hiding friends and family members and helping to secure their escape? More than thirty Jews had been hidden in Henry Skjær's Snekkersten house; surely it made sense, did it not, to suspect that Edgar Hiller had been one of them?

It seemed to Michele Wassard Larsen as well as to Ira Brilliant far away in Phoenix that at last the long-elusive pieces of the puzzle were falling into place. Surely Edgar Hiller had fled to Denmark with the lock of Beethoven's hair among his few possessions; surely he had been befriended by his musical colleague Henry Skjær; surely he had given the hair to Dr. Fremming as he struggled to flee to Sweden. It all fit perfectly except for a single and very troublesome fact: at the massive Danish national archives in Copenhagen known as the Rigsarkivet, there was no evidence that Edgar Hiller or anyone in his family ever had been in the country. The names of thousands of Germans who had entered Denmark—legally and illegally as well—during the 1930s and 1940s, including two dozen or so named Hiller, had been carefully cataloged, as was each individual's date of birth and the city from whence he or she had fled. But maddeningly, the birth dates and home cities of none of the immigrants named Hiller approximated those of Paul Hiller's wife or sons, and the names Sophie, Edgar, and Erwin simply did not appear in the archive.

———

AN ARCHIVIST AT THE YAD Vashem in Israel reported in October 1998 that the museum's extensive database showed no evidence that either Sophie Hiller, Edgar Hiller, or Erwin Hiller had died at the hands of the Nazis between the years 1935 and 1945. The search did confirm, however, that Selma Hiller, the first wife of Felix Hiller, Paul Hiller's eldest and illegitimate son, had died at Theriesenstadt. The Yad Vashem had collected no details about her capture or the circumstances of her death, yet it appeared certain that she had died on September 10, 1942, and therefore it would have been impossible for her to have been sent to the camp from Denmark. The sole sign of the other Hiller family members that archivist Oxana Korol was able to uncover was a Red Cross Tracing Service document that made it appear quite likely that a German Jew named Erwin Hiller, born in 1908, had sailed from Bremerhaven to New York on June 16, 1948, and this small bit of information suddenly appeared to be another potential breakthrough: if Erwin Hiller had emigrated to America, then surely he or his descendants could be located. He would be ninety by now, and although perhaps it was unlikely, he *might* still be alive; surely his children would be in any case.

But when Stan Lindaas at Salt Lake City's Heritage Consulting, a genealogical research firm, began to search for him as part of the burgeoning, multinational effort to solve the mystery of how the lock of hair had made its way out of Germany, it soon seemed as if Erwin Hiller simply had vanished the moment he stepped off the SS *Marine Flasher* and onto a Manhattan pier. The Red Cross tracing document had listed the Hebrew Immigrant Aid Society as the forty-year-old Hiller's New York address, but Lindaas was informed by HIAS officials that they had no record of an Erwin Hiller immigrating to the United States in 1948, or in any other year. Neither did two other New York–based Jewish history associations—the YIVO Institute for Jewish Research and the Leo Baeck Institute—have records pertaining to him, and searches of the federal government's Social Security, Immigration and Naturalization, and census records also proved entirely futile, as did inquiries aimed at dozens of Americans named Hiller who had posted Internet and other kinds of queries about their own genealogical backgrounds. Paul Hiller's son Erwin, an actor in Cologne when his whereabouts became unknown following his father's death, had come to America, it appeared, but then had disappeared a second time.

It wasn't until Alexander Fülling, a partner in the small research firm of Schröder & Fülling, GbR in the town of Gummersbach, near Cologne, initiated his own methodical search for evidence of Paul Hiller and his heirs that a sketchy picture of what had become of the family at last began to emerge. Although the vital-statistics register for the city of Cologne had been destroyed by Allied bombing at the end of World War II, Fülling was able to locate Paul Hiller's obituary, but he found it, to his substantial surprise, in the *Westdeutscher Beobachter*, which was the Rhineland's leading pro-Nazi newspaper early in 1934. Equally surprising were the bold cross placed at the top of the boxed obituary—a type that clearly had been purchased by family members or friends—as well as its repeated statements about the deceased man's devout Christianity. Hiller might have become a Christian, of course, but it seemed virtually unimaginable that he would have embraced Nazi politics in addition. Fülling could not be positive, but he strongly suspected that the obituary had been expressly designed to help hide his survivors' Jewish identities.

Slowly, incrementally, and occasionally only because of a good bit of luck, Fülling discovered more shards of information during the course of the first half of 1999: Paul Hiller had bequeathed his father's letters and diaries to the Cologne city archive, but his musical legacy—handwritten scores, sketches, and memorabilia—had been given to the combined city and university library in Ferdinand Hiller's home city of Frankfurt by his daughter Tony. Felix Hiller, Paul Hiller's eldest son—who had died in Berlin in 1963, Fülling discovered—had married Selma Hiller in 1896, then had married a woman named Johanna Fuchs in 1936, six years prior to his first wife's death, meaning that Felix and Selma certainly had divorced, although Fülling could find no record of that dissolution. Five years before Felix Hiller remarried, he had moved to Berlin from Chemnitz, and although Fülling was able to locate him in the city's 1931 *Adressbuch*—where, perhaps it shouldn't have been surprising, he was identified as a composer—he could find neither an obituary nor probate information that might have identified Felix's descendants. Next, Fülling contacted two German musicians' societies headquartered in Berlin and was informed that although their records showed no sign of a Felix Hiller, an Edgar Hiller, born in Cologne in 1906, had belonged to a sister organization in Switzerland. That Edgar

Hiller was Felix Hiller's half brother, it now seemed certain, and people at the Swiss organization were able to confirm that he had been a member during the years he lived in Zurich. The organization had lost touch with him after 1953, however, the Swiss contacts reported to Fülling, at which time he resided in Germany again, this time in the city of Hamburg.

German privacy laws make the kind of open-ended research that Alexander Fülling was undertaking a difficult process in the best of circumstances, and bureaucrats in Hamburg are notoriously far more restrictive than most, but Fülling's repeated pleas for assistance nonetheless proved successful at last, and in June 1999 he quite remarkably was able to ascertain—with the vital help of a young, understanding, and rule-bending court clerk—that Edgar Hiller had died in Hamburg on November 20, 1959, that he had never married and had had no children, and that his small estate had been willed to his brother, who lived in Los Angeles, California, and whose name was Marcel Hillaire.

It was extraordinary news—at least it was to the knot of people on two continents who had been searching for Paul Hiller's sons, or his sons' descendants, for nearly four years by now—and at last researcher Stan Lindaas in Salt Lake City could begin to make substantial progress, and he did so almost immediately: American Marcel Hillaire had been born in Cologne on April 23, 1908, just as Erwin Hiller had; he had emigrated from Germany on June 15, 1948, and that date matched Erwin Hiller's emigration record as well; he had lived in New York City, working as a Broadway and television actor until 1954, when he had moved to Los Angeles to establish his film career.

He had lived in California until his death on January 1, 1988, when he had died from complications following surgery. Like his brother Edgar, he never had married and neither did he have children, but Lindaas found that his death certificate had been signed by a woman named Esther Taylor, who had listed her relationship to the decedent as "friend," and who continued to live at the same Burbank address where she had lived eleven years before.

Since he first had heard the distressingly sketchy but nonetheless fascinating story that the lock of Beethoven's hair somehow had left the Hiller family in the midst of the Second World War and had come into the possession of a kindly Danish physician, Ira Brilliant had longed one day to speak with and perhaps even meet face-to-face one of Paul Hiller's descendants. And although Esther Taylor was not a blood relation of the man whose name had become Marcel Hillaire, Brilliant soon learned that she had become his heir, in fact. And the kind and engaging wife and mother of two young sons was nothing less than astonished when her telephone rang in early July and she began to reply in the affirmative to a series of exceedingly unanticipated questions: Yes, Marcel Hillaire had been her dear friend until his death. Yes, the actor had been born Erwin Hiller and had been raised in Cologne. Yes, his father had been Paul Hiller, the music journalist, and yes, of course, she affirmed, Marcel had told her many times about the lock of hair his father possessed, one that his famed grandfather had cut from the corpse of the greatest composer Europe ever had known.

THE TWENTY HAIRS FROM BEETHOVEN'S head that had been in Dr. Werner Baumgartner's care arrived at the Health Research Institute in Naperville, Illinois, at the end of May 1996, together with a detailed description of each peregrinating hair. Baumgartner noted that the sample he had examined and now was passing along contained two distinct "populations"—ten hairs were 5–7 centimeters in length, and ten more were 10–12 centimeters long. Positing an average growth rate of 1.3 centimeters per month, the Los Angeles scientist estimated that because of the varying lengths, the hairs had grown between four and a half and nine months prior to the composer's death. The short group contained two gray hairs, the longer group five, and the remaining thirteen hairs were dark brown.

They arrived at Dr. William Walsh's research facility—encased in a plastic vial that was protected by an outer vial as well—just as Amy Stevens's article at last appeared on the front page of the *Wall Street Journal* and immediately elicited a flood of media interest in the scientists' pursuits. Although Baumgartner spoke by telephone with a few reporters in Los Angeles, it was Walsh who met with them en masse in the Chicago suburb, both scientists and their colleagues in Arizona hoping collectively that they could offer the media a bone of sorts for a day, or two at most, then be left alone again for the long stretch of time that the new tests would require.

"I was astonished at the result," Baumgartner told the Associated Press of the morphine tests. "It's extremely strange that Beethoven, who suffered all his life, didn't take opiates. . . . Among Beethoven scholars, there is a major mystery how people can transcend great pain and create profound music. The answer is, it takes a profound person. . . . Beethoven did not choose to take something that would dehumanize him, because morphine is, after all, a loss of human freedom and human will." But Beethoven scholar William Meredith, director of the Beethoven Center, interpreted the chemist's finding rather differently. He too had been greatly surprised by the result, yet what it foremost signaled to him was the new knowledge that Beethoven "suffered needlessly" at the end of his life, especially considering that his abdomen had been opened repeatedly to drain excess fluid. "It underscores the fact that Beethoven received barbaric treatment, even by the standards of the day," Meredith told the San Jose *Mercury News*.

The man who stepped in front of the rack of microphones in Naperville offered nothing in the way of interpretive comment because his work had yet to begin, of course. But Bill Walsh did announce that in the coming months he would recommend to Guevara and Brilliant what further tests were likely to yield the most new information, and who would be the best people to perform them. He could not be sure yet how many examinations ultimately would be undertaken, but he would focus his investigations in three arenas: microscopic analysis might be employed in hopes of reaching a substantive conclusion about the hair's age and condition; trace-metal analysis, done with very modern microscopes, could search for abnormal concentrations of an array of metals; and genetic testing, if conducted, might provide insights into genetic disorders as well as establish a baseline for comparison with other Beethoven remains.

In the days following the press conferences, Beethoven's hair did indeed briefly enter the American media spotlight. The Chicago *Tribune,* Los Angeles *Times,* and San Francisco *Chronicle* all took rather sober approaches to the news the scientists had generated, while the often-outlandish New York *Post* seized the opportunity to poke some fun: "Hiller held onto the hair for years, finally giving it to his son Paul as a 30th birthday gift. ('Gee, thanks, Dad, but I was really hoping for a piece of Mozart's sports-jacket.')" The television news departments at ABC, CBS, and NBC aired segments about the impending testing and the Arizona men who had set it in motion, and in the succeeding days, Ira Brilliant logged nineteen calls from still more news organizations in the United States, Great Britain, Italy, and Japan. Beethoven's hair and its end-of the-century scrutiny were big news, but only for a moment, before other events cast them in shadow again, before Bill Walsh proceeded with the slow and orderly analyses that would occupy some of his time and much of his fascination for four more years to come.

A chemical engineer by training, William Walsh had become the leading expert on hair analysis in the United States almost by accident. While completing his Ph.D. at Iowa State University in the early 1960s, he had designed and built a high-vacuum X-ray spectrometer for trace-metal analysis for the Institute for Atomic Research in Ames. Already, he had been employed at the Los Alamos Scientific Laboratory in New Mexico and the University of Michigan Research Institute, designing and operating an array of nuclear-fuels experiments, and, once his doctoral work was done, he had accepted a position at Argonne National Laboratory near Chicago, where he directed a team of scientists whose projects focused on nuclear-fuels processing and the development of small and sophisticated batteries. It was during the two decades that Walsh had spent at Argonne that volunteer work he had undertaken in the Prisoner Assistance Program at nearby Stateville Prison had led to an obsession with the question of whether there might be a direct relationship between human chemical imbalances and antisocial behavior, a personal inquiry that soon would change his life.

In working with men who were about to be paroled, Walsh had heard repeatedly from parents and family members that the particular inmate to whom they were related had been "different" from birth, and his siblings often had been reported to be well adjusted and successful in comparison. Personal observation similarly had led Walsh to suspect that many criminals were dissimilar from the general population not so much morally or psychologically but *physiologically*, and in 1975 he and a group of volunteers he enlisted from among his colleagues at Argonne had begun to study the biochemistry of Stateville inmates in an effort to explore the question. Taking blood and urine samples from a large prison population, then removing them to laboratories for analysis, would have been difficult for many reasons, but samples of inmates' hair, on the other hand, had been relatively easy to obtain and transport, and, as Walsh and his colleagues soon had discovered, scalp hair also proved to be an excellent indicator of chemical levels retained in tissue throughout the body. By 1980, two separate Walsh-led studies—one involving ninety-six violent prison inmates and parolees and an equal number of nonviolent "control" subjects; the other a comparison of twenty-four pairs of brothers, one a violent "delinquent," his sibling a verifiable "all-American boy"—had shown similar and remarkable results. Not only had the hair of virtually all the criminal subjects evidenced abnormal levels of several essential trace metals, those elements had been present in high and low concentrations in two readily identifiable patterns—those who exhibited only periodic unexplained rages, and those who had become chronically sociopathic. There clearly *was* a link between antisocial behavior and body chemistry, the scientist now was convinced.

In the succeeding years, Walsh had been able to establish the world's first standards for trace-metal concentration in human hair, as well as reference normals based on a 100,000-sample database. In a collaboration begun in 1982 with Carl Pfeiffer, a physician and widely acknowledged expert on biochemical imbalances who was based in Princeton, New Jersey, Walsh had become increasingly convinced that such deficits and overloads could be successfully treated with minerals, vitamins, and amino acids. In 1986, he had left his long-held position at Argonne to establish the Health Research Institute, henceforth devoting his efforts full-time to the development of highly accurate methods for chemical screening of hair as well as allied kinds of applied research, and three years later he had founded the Pfeiffer Treatment Center—named in honor of his by-then deceased colleague—its programs targeted specifically at the evaluation and treatment of patients with an array of behavioral dysfunctions whose cause likely was one or more neuro-chemical imbalance.

By the time he was approached by Dr. Guevara about whether he would be interested in coordinating the testing of the hair from Beethoven's head, Walsh's burgeoning renown—coupled with the generally low esteem in which the field of hair analysis long had been held—had made him the scientist of choice, and by now he had participated in forensic analyses of the hair biochemistry of Charles Manson and three dozen more notorious American criminals. Ludwig van Beethoven would be Walsh's first famous—rather than infamous—subject, and that had been a key reason for his positive response to Guevara's overture. So, too, had been his enduring memory of the heirloom bust of the great composer his mother, a piano instructor, long had kept positioned on the baby grand piano in their Bay City, Michigan, home back when he was a boy.

With the consent of Dr. Guevara and Ira Brilliant, Walsh now planned to proceed very cautiously. He would perform none of the testing himself, but instead would select a group of two or three scientists whom he believed were the best of the best in their arcane areas of expertise; each scientist would be informed only that he was examining the hair of a "famous person," and Walsh would allow each one to proceed with his experiment only after he was convinced of the soundness of the scientist's methodology and his utter commitment to accuracy. All work would be performed free of charge, and Walsh therefore would agree to be very patient while each test was undertaken. The owners of the hair, in turn, had to be glacially patient as well, and two and a half years passed, in fact, before at last Walsh flew to Phoenix and presented Guevara and Brilliant with a preliminary report of the findings he had obtained, one of which, in particular, staggered the two men who so long had held the figure of the immortal Beethoven in such exalted regard.

THROUGHOUT THE CENTURY THAT WAS about to come to a close, Beethoven scholars with a focal interest in the composer's chronic ill-health—as well as physicians with particular passions for Beethoven's music—had studied his medical history and speculated about the causes of his many diseases and the impact they made on his music. American musicologist Clarence J. Blake, writing in 1901 about the composer's loss of hearing, had insisted that "there is no more pathetic picture than that of Beethoven in his later years, at an age when he should have been in the perfection of his physical manhood, deaf to overwhelming applause or striking in tumultuous discord the piano which to him was dumb." Yet despite that expression of empathy, it had appeared to Blake that Beethoven's hearing deficit had not, in fact, influenced his compositions in a significant way. "Indeed it may be questioned," Blake had concluded his short essay, "if his musical nature were affected at all other than favorably by his infirmity. His art was greater than the man, or rather the man in his art was greater than himself."

By midcentury, scholars such as Waldemar Schweisheimer

had grown willing to argue that the composer's deafness had influenced his music profoundly, in fact, and even to posit its cause. "Beethoven's tragic deafness was the consequence of a disease of the inner ear, a *neuritis acoustica*. The most probable cause of this neuritis was a severe early attack of typhoid fever," Schweisheimer had written in the *Musical Quarterly* in 1945.

The possibility that the hearing loss had been caused instead by syphilis—a theory that had grown popular in some circles—simply could not be supported by Beethoven's medical history, according to Schweisheimer, who described the claim that he had syphilis as "pure invention," and it had been utterly discredited more than a century before, he believed, when none of several vivid and telltale signs of the disease had been observed at autopsy. A quarter century later, however, the notion that syphilis had been the composer's chief medical culprit nonetheless had grown commonplace enough that British scholar Edward Larkin had devoted an entire section of his long essay, "Beethoven's Medical History," to its refutation. Like Schweisheimer, Larkin had not intended to protect Beethoven's magisterial reputation by refusing to acknowledge the possibility of his having contracted a venereal disease; in fact, he believed it was probable that he had: "It is likely that Beethoven, like everybody else, caught gonorrhea," Larkin had written, his essay published in 1970 as an appendix to *Beethoven: The Last Decade*, by Martin Cooper, "but there is no evidence that either his lifelong illnesses or his deafness were syphilitic, and the substantial medical writers make other diagnoses."

For his part, Larkin suspected that Beethoven's deafness most probably was caused by otosclerosis, the hardening of the cartilaginous opening to the inner ear. The composer's lifelong litany of other disorders—"hepatitis, colitis, rheumatism, repeated catarrhs, abscesses, cryopathy (attacks precipitated by chilling), the opthalmia and the skin disorders"—Larkin believed could be seen as symptomatic and "extremely suggestive of connective tissue immunopathy," a disorder in which disease-fighting antibodies strangely and selectively attempt to destroy the body's own bone, cartilage, ligaments, tendons, or soft tissue. When British rheumatologist and Beethoven devotee Thomas Palferman had weighed in on the etiology of Beethoven's diseases in a comprehensive article published in the Beethoven Center's *Beethoven Journal* in 1992, he had noted the several previous diagnoses, and had agreed with Larkin that an "autoimmune" disorder might have been at the root of most of Beethoven's maladies. Yet it wasn't likely that it had caused his hearing loss as well, and Palferman therefore had suggested his own unprecedented diagnosis.

Sarcoidosis, a disease closely related to tuberculosis and characterized by the appearance of noncancerous, tumorlike growths on organs throughout the body—neoplasms capable of inflicting severe damage and its attendant pain—was the one disease Palferman believed could encompass every aspect of Beethoven's medical misfortune. Although often self-limiting and rather benign in its effects, a severe case of sarcoidosis, Palferman had contended, could account for the destroyed liver that ended Beethoven's life, for his eye complaints, his frequent respiratory attacks; and the kidney stones discovered at autopsy also could explain his chronic and often crippling abdominal pain. And although it was reported in the medical literature only extremely rarely, the British physician had admitted, sarcoidosis could also lead to deafness. It was the sole diagnosis that could provide a unified explanation of the great man's extensive suffering, and countering what Clarence Blake had written nearly a century before, Palferman had concluded his argument by suggesting that because "pain and despair can amplify artistic originality, it is perhaps axiomatic that Beethoven's many adversities allowed him to plumb emotional depths that a more tranquil life would have denied him." Put simply, Beethoven's diseases therefore had played an inspiriting role in the creation of his profoundly emotive music.

It appears that Philip Weiss, a contributing writer for the *New York Times Magazine* did not read Palferman's commentary or any of those that had preceded it when he took up the subject of Beethoven's health and the ongoing study of Beethoven's hair in October 1998. The reporter had seized upon Ira Brilliant and Che Guevara as examples of amateurs out of their depths in the burgeoning arena of forensic history in an article published in the *New York Times Magazine* on November 30, and Weiss was sure as well that he had ferreted out the reason why the two men had bought the lock of hair, then gone to great lengths to have it tested: they were out to prove that Beethoven had contracted syphilis. Although each man had insisted to Weiss that the ongoing hair analysis was aimed at no predetermined goal when he had visited Brilliant at the Beethoven Center in San Jose and Guevara in Nogales, the writer would not be deterred, and the result was a story entitled "Beethoven's Hair Tells All!," the cover of the magazine illustrated with an image of the composer seated at his piano and glaring at the tabloid *"Vienna Confidential,"* whose headline blared, "Clap for Beethoven? His hair says it all: He's got V.D."

Although Weiss conceded that Brilliant was a "charming 76-year-old," he also depicted him as a man blindly determined to have his way. Guevara, in turn, was someone of whom the writer could crow, "I recognized his type. He was the well-read provincial doctor. . . . His theories of history owed a lot to Gore Vidal novels and correspondence videos." And the tests the two men had authorized William Walsh to undertake—examinations Weiss was certain were aimed at shouting to the world that Beethoven had been sexually indiscreet—struck him "as rather gee-whiz and trivial."

Neither Guevara nor Brilliant took pleasure in being portrayed in the nation's leading newspaper as something of a syphilis-obsessed bumpkin, and, what was worse was the fact that the Beethoven cognoscenti around the world now might presume that they were bent on buttressing a medical diagnosis that had been soundly discredited for nearly three decades. The magazine writer wrongly had presumed—then had presented it as cleverly uncovered inside information—that the owners of the Guevara lock had their sights set on syphilis yet were too coy to admit it publicly. The doctor was a *urologist*, after all, Weiss reminded the *Times's* readers.

Yet as the timing by chance would have it, Ira Brilliant and Dr. Guevara had met with testing coordinator William Walsh in Arizona during the five weeks between their conversations with Weiss and the article's appearance, and they now were privy to information that only Walsh hitherto had known: Beethoven's hair had evidenced levels of mercury so low they were undetectable. Mercury had been a ubiquitous treatment for syphilis and dozens of other infections early in the nineteenth century, one the composer certainly would have consumed regularly if he knowingly had been battling the disease. Syphilis now clearly could not explain Beethoven's cruel concert of diseases. But Bill Walsh and the men he had employed to test the hair had found something else that might.

ESTHER TAYLOR KNEW THAT A lock of Beethoven's hair had been in her dear friend's family for two generations, but she could not explain how it had reached Denmark, nor could she name the person who had given it away.

A twenty-year-old pulmonary therapist working at Brotman Memorial Hospital in Culver City, California, she had met Marcel Hillaire in the spring of 1974, just days after he had been thrown high in the air by a speeding automobile as he was attempting to cross La Brea Avenue at Hollywood Boulevard. Hillaire's injuries were extensive; he had been hospitalized for four months, and during that time Esther Taylor had grown enchanted by the debonair European man, and he, in turn, by her. Despite the four decades that separated their ages, the two grew very close, and when at last he was released from the hospital, Esther Taylor and Marcel Hillaire found an apartment on Burnside Avenue in Los Angeles that they were sure would suit them both, one which they shared for the following eight years. Marcel Hillaire had led a rich yet often chaotic life, Esther learned early on, and she loved to hear his magical stories about his youth. He had been born Erwin Ottmar Hiller in Cologne on April 23, 1908. His mother was Sophie Lion, a lieder singer who always lamented the fact that the Lion branch of her ancient tribe somehow had settled in Germany. His father was a proud patriot who wore a Kaiser Wilhelm mustache, but he was a passionate socialist as well, and although he once had directed the city's opera, Paul Hiller had worked as a newspaper's music critic by the time Erwin and his elder brother Edgar came along. His paternal grandfather, who had died long before he was born, had been Cologne's *Kapellmeister* for many years; his father still possessed a few precious mementos that once had belonged to the famed Ferdinand: there was a copy of the death mask that had been shaped from clay pressed onto the deceased Ludwig van Beethoven's face; there was a weathered conductor's baton that had belonged to Beethoven—or had it been his grandfather's friend Felix Mendelssohn's baton? Or was it merely his grandfather's own? He couldn't be sure—and secure under the glass of a small black locket was a bit of hair his grandfather had clipped from Beethoven's head.

Esther Taylor was sure Marcel would have been hugely helpful in explaining how the lock of hair had left his family and had traveled to Denmark—sadly, she never had dreamed that a decade after his death people would seek her out in hopes that she had information about Marcel's distant past, and about that lock of hair. And she was certain of something more: Marcel had been unhappy that the lock of hair went to a museum—as he had been told it had—rather than to him or his brother Edgar.

In a renewed attempt to ascertain where the hair had gone when it left the Hiller's home at 31 Eifelstrasse in Cologne—and armed now with Esther Taylor's vital information—German researcher Alexander Fülling began again to search, this time for evidence of the lock of hair itself rather than for Felix Hiller, dead since 1963, or his half brother Edgar, who had died in Hamburg in 1959, or for Erwin, who had become Marcel Hillaire. But what Fülling ultimately found merely were more dead ends: the Cologne music academy that Ferdinand Hiller had directed for decades had no record of a gift from his son of a lock of Beethoven's hair; neither did the city archive, nor the public library, nor the library of the university, and although the collection of the Beethoven-Archiv in Bonn included several locks of the master's hair, none had been the gift of Paul Hiller, and none had been spirited to Denmark during the war.

Ferdinand Hiller's diaries and letters, however, *had* been bequeathed to the music academy, and from archivists there Fülling learned that Paul Hiller's sister Tony also had given much of her father's musical legacy—sketches, manuscripts, and scores—to the museum of the combined public and university library in Frankfurt. Surely it was worth inquiring whether the lock of hair had been sequestered there, Fülling decided, and he briefly was stunned in the fall of 1999 when he was informed by archivist Ann Kersting-Meuleman that the museum once had possessed a lock of Beethoven's hair, which she believed had been unaccounted for after the war. The following morning, however, the telephone was ringing as Fülling opened his office door; it was Kersting-Meuleman, calling from Frankfurt, with an apology. The lock of hair in question still was in the museum's possession—she was looking at it as she spoke, in fact—and it had been among the many notable items that had been acquired when Frankfurter Friedrich Nicholas Manskopf willed the collection of his private music history museum to the city in 1929.

So there it was: Marcel Hillaire had told Esther Taylor repeatedly during the years she lived with him that his father had given the venerable hair that once had been Beethoven's to an institution of some sort, where Paul Hiller had expected it to be cared for in perpetuity. Yet why could Fülling find no evidence of the generous gift despite extensive searching? That question seemed to spawn a number of plausible answers: perhaps Marcel Hillaire chose to claim that the lock of hair had been given away because his knowledge of what actually had become of it was enduringly painful. It is imaginable as well that Paul Hiller told his son that he had given the lock of hair to a museum when, in fact, he had given it to his brother Edgar or to someone outside their immediate family. Perhaps, on the other hand, Fülling simply had yet to make an inquiry at the proper museum, a possibility that seemed increasingly unlikely; Paul Hiller had lived in Cologne throughout his life, and his father had been much beloved in that city for more than thirty years; surely it was there beside the Rhine, or in nearby Bonn, that Paul Hiller would have wanted the lock of hair to remain. Was a written record of the gift destroyed in the massive Allied bombing at the end of the Second World War? Much of Cologne had been leveled in 1945; whole libraries had been decimated and scores of materials in the city's central archive simply had ceased to exist; perhaps a document pertaining to Paul Hiller's bequest had been destroyed in the conflagration. Or, did someone—a museum employee, a museum trustee perhaps—who had access to the lock of hair and who had taken it as he or she fled Germany, take as well the printed evidence that proved the hair had been in the institution's possession in the first place? If the lock of hair had been stolen—either by someone who wanted it solely for its monetary value, or by someone who refused to leave it behind for the hated Nazis—surely that person might have destroyed whatever records once had signaled its existence. Was it someone who had known Paul Hiller or his family who absconded from Cologne with a hidden lock of hair? Did the person who ultimately gave the hair to Dr. Fremming know precisely where it had come from, or had the black locket with the bit of Beethoven inside been used as barter and been passed from hand to hand a dozen times before it reached the town of Gilleleje? Could answers to those questions ever be ascertained? Could they ultimately be mined in much the same way that a small team of American scientists recently had gleaned secrets about Beethoven's health from his 170-year-old hair? Or would the passage of Beethoven's hair to Denmark always remain a perplexing mystery?

———

WILLIAM WALSH, LIKE WERNER BAUMGARTNER before him, wanted the men with whom he met privately in Arizona to know that it had been his honor to coordinate the several examinations of Beethoven's hair. Yet it was important to him that he made it clear as well that his foremost interest along the way had been in ensuring that good science had been performed during the preceding twenty-nine months. Neither his nor his colleagues' careers could be advanced in any way by shoddy methodology or sloppy lab procedures. He had worked too hard for too many years in legitimizing hair analysis and proving its important applications to risk future accusations that he had been searching for notoriety, rather than whatever truth lay trapped in the twenty strands of hair. But once he had made those perspectives clear, however, Walsh next wanted the owners of Beethoven's hair to know that he had riveting information for them, which he had summarized in a seven-page report.

Following their arrival from Los Angeles in May 1996, Walsh had dried the hairs—still wet from Baumgartner's radioimmunoassay procedure—in his lab at the Health Research Institute, then had forwarded two hairs, one brown, one gray, to Max Adams, an expert in high-magnification forensics and photomicrography who lives on a yacht that sails the Caribbean. Adams had studied the hairs at magnifications of 100X, 400X, and 1,000X, and had found, not surprisingly, that the hair had begun to deteriorate. "Several areas had experienced erosion of the outer keratin layer and numerous tiny hair fragments were observed," Walsh wrote in the confidential report. But the hair had not disintegrated, as it certainly might have by now, and its overall condition surely owed much to its long-term storage between the sealed pieces of glass. Although Adams had been able to determine that "gaseous elements with high diffusion coefficients, such as oxygen" had permeated the hair, he was certain that the keratin layer on the outside of each hair shaft remained intact enough to have prohibited the penetration of heavy metal atoms. In other words, it had been Adams's opinion that whatever metals might later be found in the sampled hair had not entered it after Beethoven's death.

Fourteen months had passed following Adams's examination before Walsh at last determined what he believed would be the best method and the best person for trace-metal analysis, and Walter McCrone, the indefatigable eighty-three-year-old founder of the McCrone Research Institute in Chicago, was that man. Likely still the nation's foremost chemical microscopist despite his aggregate years, it was McCrone who had demonstrated conclusively in the 1980s that the Shroud of Turin had been painted in the fourteenth century and was not, therefore, the burial cloth of Jesus; and prior to that determination, McCrone also had proven—by examining a sample of *his* hair—that Napoleon had not died from arsenic poisoning, as long had been suspected.

In his examination of the two Beethoven hairs, McCrone first had incinerated each one, as well as three more control hairs taken from living persons, in a low-temperature nascent oxygen asher. The ash from each of the five hairs subsequently had been analyzed using both scanning electron microscope energy dispersion spectrometry, known as SEM/EDS, and scanning ion microscope mass spectrometry, SIMS—each technique employing atomic interactions and quantum physics rather than light and magnification to "peer inside" a test material.

Not long after he had received the hairs, McCrone had returned to Walsh chemical data pertaining to a total of fifty-three separate elements, although not every one of those had been found in measurable quantities in each of the five samples. Walsh, in turn, had analyzed independently the raw results, explaining in his report that "evaluation of trace elements in hair can be quite complex, and requires knowledge of metal metabolism, nutrient transport, excretion kinetics, bile shunting, and many other biochemical processes and factors." The examinations by electron microscopy ultimately had been unable to encounter any evidence in either the Beethoven samples or the controls of the elevated copper/zinc ratio, together with very high levels of sodium and potassium, that repeatedly Walsh had found in the hair of people of extreme intelligence; neither Beethoven nor any of the three controls had exhibited that "genius pattern," he had determined. All five samples, in fact, had shown normal concentrations of a total of forty-three elements. The three control samples had exhibited normal lead concentrations as well, but the two Beethoven samples dramatically had not—and that was the information that Walsh now was eager to share: the three controls had shown relative lead concentrations of 0.95, 1.4, and 9.8, whereas the relative concentrations in the Beethoven samples, in comparison, had been as high as 90 and 250.

It was an absolutely arresting finding, one that meant that the average amount of lead in the Beethoven hair had been *forty-two times* the lead average contained in the controls. Ludwig van Beethoven, Walsh believed the evidence now strongly suggested, had been massively toxic with lead at the time of his death and may have been for dozens of years before.

NEITHER CHE GUEVARA NOR IRA Brilliant ever had dared to presume that the analysis they had set in motion three years before ultimately would lead to compelling new information about Beethoven's health, let alone a comprehensive explanation of why his body so long had been so burdened. Yet suddenly that outcome appeared possible. Lead no longer poisoned children and adults as commonly as it once had, but in the years before its very deleterious effects on the human body had become intimately understood, lead in cookware, tableware, and water pipes—among myriad sources—had poisoned millions of people around the world, sometimes only subtly, but often with disastrous results.

The physiological effects of lead poisoning in children have been widely understood and discussed throughout most of the twentieth century, but the metal is capable of devastating adults as well, and a catalog of its common clinical manifestations—a condition called plumbism—does, very intriguingly, read like a somber list of Beethoven's lifelong ills. Chronic toxic exposure to lead almost invariably causes intermittent yet long-term gastrointestinal distress characterized by severe abdominal cramping, vomiting, constipation and/or diarrhea; gout is common, as are a variety of rheumatic complaints, and so too are skin pallor and jaundice. Recurrent headaches, loss of appetite, irritability, forgetfulness, and erratic behavior often are reported in adults with plumbism, as is a generalized kind of clumsiness caused by the partial paralysis of extensor muscles of the arms and legs. Other neurological symptoms that are widely acknowledged in the medical literature—but which certainly are not common to every case—are visual deficits and a progressive loss of hearing caused by permanent damage to the optic and auditory nerves.

Compare those dramatically debilitating symptoms with a synopsis of the composer's ailments over the course of his lifetime, one that was compiled by Drs. Hans Bankl and Hans Jesserer of the University of Vienna's Institute for the History of Medicine in their 1986 book *Die Krankheiten Ludwig van Beethovens* (The Illnesses of Ludwig van Beethoven). In 1795, the twenty-four-year-old composer began to experience frequent and often intense abdominal pains; in 1798, he first became aware of a troublesome inability to hear what people said, and soon he also began to experience buzzing and ringing in his ears. In 1801, Beethoven constantly was plagued with diarrhea, fever, and abdominal cramping, and those complaints continued for the succeeding decade; he had several teeth pulled in 1807 in the hope that the extractions would relieve his recurrent "gouty headaches"; his hearing continued to diminish, and he often was forced to keep cotton in his ears in order to reduce "unpleasant rustling" sounds, or tinnitus. Although his intestinal ailments lessened between the years of 1811 and 1816, they then returned with a vengeance, as did "frightful attacks of rheumatism" that culminated in a serious rheumatic fever in 1820 that sent him to bed for six weeks. Beethoven experienced an attack of jaundice and more acute diarrhea and constipation in 1821, a "gout of my chest" in 1822, persistent eye pain and still more "wretched" cramping in 1823—his hearing already so poor for the preceding five years that people with whom he was in contact had begun to write down whatever they wanted him to know. He was frequently bedridden in 1824, and in 1825 his bowels became inflamed, his nose bled often, and he vomited regularly as well. His abdomen began to swell a year later; he had severe back pain, grew terribly jaundiced, suffered a bout of pneumonia, and at the end of that year, he slid into a final illness that culminated three months later in a "coma hepaticum," his death directly induced by the failure of his liver. In addition to those aggregate illnesses, the composer indeed often was irritable and erratic in his behavior; beginning in 1800, he told friends that he had begun to consume a substantial amount of wine with meals in the hope that it would stimulate his increasingly poor appetite, as well as ease his pain. Even the notoriously unusual way in which he walked also is suggestive of the effects of chronic lead toxicity.

The very high lead levels that Walter McCrone detected in Beethoven's hair are strictly indicative only of the fact that Beethoven was massively lead toxic in the last months of his life, of course, yet given his thirty years of mounting illnesses, his testy behavior and chronic clumsiness, it now appears very probable that he had consumed large amounts of lead long before. It is possible that in 1795 or thereabouts, Beethoven somehow ingested a massive quantity of lead only a single time; lead is quickly deposited in bone, where it readily resides for many years, and from which source it subsequently is slowly released back into the body. On the other hand, he may have been insidiously poisoned by the same source of lead throughout the course of the last half of his life. Although the restless Beethoven moved constantly during those years, among the possessions that were auctioned following his death were "14 china plates, some earthenware, 1 tin cup, several glasses, bottles and bowls, 4 brass candleholders, 1 brass mortar, 1 copper tub, 1 rotisserie, assorted iron pots and pans, and the usual kitchen furnishings." That earthenware certainly can be suspected of containing a leaden glaze; the china might have as well, and the "tin" cup and "iron" pots also could have been the cause. It seems unlikely, given his many residences, that lead-soldered water pipes poisoned Beethoven severely yet somehow spared the remaining citizens of Vienna, but the fact that he consumed considerable amounts of wine, which in that era often was "plumbed" with lead to lessen its bitterness—a practice that even then was strongly discouraged because the consumption of plumbed wine so clearly led to "the colic"— also means that wine cannot be ruled out as a possible source of the poison.

WHILE THEY REMAINED TOGETHER IN Tucson in the autumn of 1998, Bill Walsh, Ira Brilliant, and Che Guevara collectively agreed as they began to discuss how best to make their findings public that it would be virtually impossible ever to positively identify what had caused the lead levels in Beethoven's hair to exceed forty times the contemporary norm. And neither did the three men believe they should announce that they plainly had solved a centuries-old mystery about the cause of the composer's deafness and the source of his chronic ill health as well. Yet they had set in motion the testing of the hair three years before specifically in hopes that new information about the composer's death and troubled life could be ascertained, and now it appeared, rather remarkably, that their simple goal had been achieved.

Although one reporter had charged that they were bent on tabloid salacity, instead it had been cautious and open-ended science that had shaped the testing's course. Guevara, a clinical physician who had studied his craft for fourteen years and now had practiced it for an equal length of time, and Walsh, who had had to struggle hard to achieve his own acclaim, now foremost believed that the announcement of their findings had to be cradled in circumspection, and Brilliant agreed with them. Guevara and Walsh would coauthor a paper and submit it to a scientific journal for publication, they ultimately decided. Their article would detail the analytical methodologies and laboratory procedures that they had employed; it would recount Walter McCrone's arresting finding; it would cite studies that had been presented in similar sorts of articles during the preceding quarter of the century demonstrating lead's ability to cause debilitating hearing deficits; and they would, of course, compare Beethoven's medical history to the concert of symptoms that plumbism commonly induces. But just as British rheumatologist Thomas Palferman had done when he proposed sarcoidosis as a unified diagnosis of the composer's many maladies in the *Beethoven Journal* in 1992, they also would acknowledge that Beethoven could have been poisoned by lead and still have suffered unrelated diseases as well.

Yet Palferman himself had explained that the search for a single cause of diffuse complaints is an honored medical tradition. "The Franciscan philosopher William of Occam . . . has been credited with the dictum *Entia non sunt multiplicanda praeter necessitatem* (Entities should not be multiplied except when necessary). Applied to medicine, the principle of Occam's Razor encourages the intellectual discipline of seeking relentlessly a unifying diagnosis, no matter how obscure or unrelated the many aspects of a clinical problem might appear." Given Palferman's own areas of expertise and the information available at the time, it was sarcoidosis that for him came closest to providing that unifying explanation of the great composer's complaints. But it was Beethoven's deafness that had been hardest to explain in that context, a point underscored by Scottish gastroenterologist Adam Kubba and music historian Madeleine Young in their "medical biography" of Beethoven published in *The Lancet* in January 1996, just as the testing of hair from the Guevara lock had commenced. "Though a good explanation for his eye conditions, sarcoidosis could not account for Beethoven's deafness," they had written. "He would have had to have developed neurosarcoidosis with all its associated neurological deficits for it to have caused loss of hearing."

Kubba and Young similarly had discounted Edward Larkin's

1970 suggestion that a connective tissue disease accounted for all of Beethoven's disorders save the deafness; and neither were they convinced that Paget's disease of bone, tuberculosis, inflammatory bowel disease, or Whipple's disease—each suggested as a unifying cause at some point during the century that was drawing to a rapid close—were, in fact, the collective cause. The two Scots had concluded their analysis by expressing their personal beliefs that Beethoven's agonizingly poor health surely was rooted in multiple disease processes, but the three Americans who now possessed vital new information— the news that Beethoven's hair had exhibited lead levels that were startlingly high—were eager to learn what commentators like Kubba and Young, Palferman, and a score of others would make of the proposition that plumbism, in fact, explained Beethoven's life of trouble best of all.

Walsh wanted to go one step further. He knew that if bone remains of Beethoven existed, by some remote chance, testing performed on them would buttress enormously the results of the hair analysis; and moreover, if hair and bone then were compared by DNA sequencing and were determined irrefutably to have come from the same human being, then the case they could make for the accuracy of their work and the likelihood that chronic plumbism explained very much of the composer's medical history would become a compelling one indeed. As it happened, Drs. Bankl and Jesserer in Vienna had examined small fragments of Beethoven's skull in the mid-1980s in the course of the research for their book. More than a century before, the bones had been sequestered by an anthropologist who had examined the composer's skeletal remains after his corpse had been exhumed; they had been loaned for the latter-day study by an aging Frenchman, who had inherited them from his great-uncle, that same anthropologist. Perhaps, just perhaps, Brilliant suggested, the Frenchman could be persuaded to have them examined again.

IT HAD BEEN FOUR YEARS since the two Beethoven enthusiasts from Arizona had acquired a lock of the great man's hair, then had begun to contemplate whether they might ask scientists to see what secrets it would shed. It had been four years as well since they first had heard the sketchy and mysterious story of how the lock of hair had been passed from Ferdinand Hiller to his son, then somehow had traveled to Denmark, where it was made a gift in the town of Gilleleje. Although the hair in recent days had led them toward a satisfying new conclusion about why Beethoven had suffered so long, the two men and their colleagues still were frustrated by the way in which the hair's whereabouts in the months that had led to October 1943 remained a conundrum.

Yes, researchers ultimately had discovered that Erwin Hiller had emigrated to America, assumed a new name, then continued his acting career; and the searching's greatest success surely had been the discovery of Esther Taylor, his heir. She had confirmed that the lock of hair had been a family heirloom, and Paul Hiller's inscription on the back of a photograph of himself that he had given to his son—a photograph Esther Taylor now cherished—had proved beyond any doubt that it was Paul

Hiller's hand as well that had written the explanatory note on the back of the black locket. Esther Taylor too had been able to explain that Erwin—her Marcel—had remained in Germany and France during the war, and had not traveled to Denmark; and it was she as well who had offered the fresh insight that Marcel believed his father had given the lock of hair to a museum sometime before his death.

Sophie Hiller died in Cologne in 1942, researcher Alexander Fülling had discovered, and therefore it appeared that she, like Erwin, had remained in Germany rather than flee to Denmark. Her son Edgar, the opera singer whose promising career had been shattered by the war, had lived in Zurich from 1939 until 1948, when he briefly had followed his brother to the United States before eventually settling again in Hamburg. Although it was conceivable that he had traveled to Denmark during those years, it now seemed unlikely, particularly considering that the Nazis had occupied the country during most of those years and that he had been a Jew. If Marcel's information was correct, someone else had stolen the locket from an unknown German institution, then had spirited it to Denmark—taking it because it was a vital relic that somehow had to be preserved, or perhaps merely pilfering it as a kind of booty that one day might be quite convenient.

In Denmark, a dozen people had attempted to solve the enduring enigma by now. Author Christian Tortzen, retired fisherman Julius Jørgensen, historian Therkel Stræde, and musicologist and Theriesenstadt survivor Paul Sandfort, in particular, had helped Michele Wassard Larsen piece together the events of the first days of October 1943. From their collective efforts, it now seemed certain that Kay and Marta Fremming had sheltered refugees in their home on those days, that Marta had been active in helping escaping Jews hide in the Gilleleje Church, and that her husband had attended to one or more of them on the night they were captured. It was far less certain, yet the available evidence nonetheless suggested, that the renowned opera baritone Henry Skjær—who had helped refugees reach the church as well—had been a key intermediary, one who somehow linked a German Jew with a precious locket in his pocket to the kindhearted physician to whom the locket subsequently had been given.

As Michele Wassard Larsen continued to search for information late in 1999, there remained a few stones for her still to overturn, although the possibility of encountering a satisfying explanation beneath one of them appeared increasingly unlikely. Paul Sandfort had explained some months before that he and his family had fled to Gilleleje on instructions from Dr. N. R. Blegvad, the Royal Theatre physician, and Michele still hoped to find a son or daughter of the doctor who might, by chance, remember hearing that his father had helped an immigrant from Germany escape as well. And there also was this: Tina Sandén, an archivist in the city of Lund in Sweden, had reported that her search of the police registers that recorded the names of everyone who had reached Sweden safely in 1943 had turned up a young German who had given his name as M. T. Teodra Hiller. His birth date was listed as October 10, 1915, and he had identified himself—quite curiously—as an actor. He had arrived in Sweden on October 7, 1943, the very day of the early-morning raid on the Gilleleje Church.

Once more Michele had encountered something new that led intriguingly to further questions. If the man's date of birth had been correct, this Hiller would have been nine years younger than Edgar Hiller, seven years Erwin's junior, and the two had had no cousins or other relatives whose birth dates would have been approximate. Yet could this be simply another extraordinary coincidence? Was it possible that a Jewish actor named Hiller—a largely "Christian" surname—had fled to Denmark, then escaped to Sweden on a day when dozens of refugees had boarded boats in Gilleleje, yet nonetheless had had nothing whatsoever to do with the now-legendary lock of hair?

It *was* possible, of course, yet the several synchronicities were haunting. Erwin Hiller, the actor, had called himself Harry Fürster for a time early in the war. Despite what seemed to be strong evidence that he had remained in Germany, did he, in fact, find his way first to Denmark, then to Sweden, where it seemed only prudent for him to continue to shield his identity? Did his brother Edgar, presumed to be in Zurich at the time, make a similar journey and similarly misidentify himself? Did someone else—who possibly would have known the provenance of the hair he had left behind in Gilleleje—find it fitting somehow to tell a sympathetic Swedish policeman that Hiller was his name?

For Michele Wassard Larsen and Thomas her son, for Ira Brilliant and Che Guevara, for Bill Meredith, Patricia Stroh and the Beethoven Center staff, and a whole coterie of people on two continents who had become captivated by this most improbable of stories, these and the larger and enveloping questions of how and where and why the venerable locket had been passed to Dr. Fremming were powerfully compelling, even if they were forever unlikely to be answered. They were questions that continued to illuminate the quiet heroism that had occurred on the coast of Denmark; they drew a resonant reference to the belief in freedom that Beethoven himself had held so dear; like the urge to discover that had spawned the forensic study of his hair, they were questions that were wonderfully worth the asking, and like his splendid music, they seemed certain to endure for much time to come.

1826~1827

By 1826, Beethoven's hair had gone quite gray. His physical strength and the vitality that long had helped him persevere were gone; his eyes continued to ache; he could hear nothing; his gut still roiled tumultuously, the pain and insidious diarrhea surely exacerbated by the fact that he had begun to drink more wine than ever before—as much as a full bottle with each meal, according to dining companions and the tavern-keepers who regularly served him.

In the hope of defeating his diseases, over the years Beethoven had sought the advice and ameliorating assistance of fifteen different physicians in Bonn and Vienna. Most of them had been "medical asses," he insisted, but it was far nearer the truth that curative medicine was merely in its infancy in those days. Early in the nineteenth century, bleeding and leeching still were commonplace, and poisonous mercury mistakenly was believed to be a panacea for dozens of disorders. Doctors attempted to make their charges comfortable and to ease their pain with morphine when they could—and the latest challenge of medicine was the simple attempt to explain the *cause* of an illness—but true cures remained largely elusive. As his several physicians had struggled to find a unified explanation for Beethoven's lifelong ills, they had queried their patient repeatedly about the years of the 1790s. The composer himself suspected that his incessant "colic" had been the cause of his deafness, and Dr. Franz Wegeler, his old friend and frequent medical adviser, also believed that both ears and bowels had been beset by the same mysterious trouble. "The seeds of his disorders, his hearing problem, and the dropsy that finally killed him, already lay within my friend's ailing body in 1796," he speculated years later, although he actually may have been remembering 1797, a year that for Beethoven was far more etched by illness than the one before it. Yet in any case, Wegeler had continued to suspect long after Beethoven's death that something insidious had befallen him in those early years, something that ultimately had been the culprit for the amalgamated troubles that ensued.

It was "dropsy"—the swelling caused by the retention of fluids that is now known as edema—that had begun to plague Beethoven while he lived with his brother in the town of Gneixendorf in the Austrian countryside late in 1826. His feet were first to balloon, and they did so very painfully; then his belly too grew fat with fluid, and by the time he and Karl, his nephew, began their journey back to Vienna on December 1, he already was nearly immobilized by these dire new symptoms. Beethoven and Karl were forced to spend a night en route home in an unheated room above a tavern, and by the time he was delivered at last to his lodgings near the university, Beethoven had developed a high fever, a hacking cough, and had a shooting pain in his side. Dr. Braunhofer, nominally still his physician, declined to attend to his patient for reasons that remain unclear; a second doctor promised to come quickly but did not, and it wasn't until their third day back in the city that Karl was able to secure the services of Dr. Andreas Wawruch, a professor of pathology and clinical medicine at the Vienna Hospital. "One who holds your name in high honor will do everything possible to bring you speedy relief," the physician scribbled into the conversation book as he was introduced at bedside to the famous man whose visage had turned yellowish and who by now had become terribly infirm, his breathing labored, blood dripping from his mouth. Although Wawruch was able to make his patient a bit more comfortable that day by administering "a severe counter-treatment for inflammation," when he arrived for his daily visit five days hence he discovered that Beethoven was near death and now also was raging at that realization:

I found him greatly disturbed and jaundiced all over his body. A frightful choleric attack had threatened his life in the preceding night. A violent rage, a great grief because of sustained ingratitude and undeserved humiliation, was the cause of this mighty explosion. Trembling and shivering, he bent double because of the pains that raged in his liver and intestines, and his feet, hitherto moderately inflated, were tremendously swollen. . . . Gentle entreaties from his friends quieted the threatening mental tempest, and the forgiving man forgot all the humiliation that had been put upon him. But the disease moved onward with giant strides.

Three weeks into the crisis, Beethoven's abdomen had become so swollen that Wawruch now believed there was no choice but to drain its fluid surgically, a procedure that was performed on December 20, and which produced literally gallons of septic, watery liquid. Beethoven was better, but only a little, when he said good-bye to Karl on January 2, 1827, as the young man left to begin his military posting in Moravia, and the following day Beethoven composed a will making Karl his sole heir. A second tapping on January 8 produced even more liquid than had been drained the first time, and now he was horribly awash in his own fluid, his bedclothes and mattress soaked, a large wooden bowl overflowing beneath his bed, the straw that was meant to protect the floor fouled as well and filled with cockroaches that had been attracted by the stench.

It was an ugly and unseemly and demeaning way to die. But although the bugs disgusted him, otherwise Beethoven now began to grow calm. He sketched music and revised the metronome markings on a score of the Ninth Symphony for his benefactors at the London Philharmonic Society, who in turn, and on hearing of his plight, made him a loan of a hundred pounds that they hoped could be applied to his medical care. From his longtime friend and frequent landlord Johann Pasqualati, he requested sweets: "Please send me some more stewed cherries today, but cooked quite simply, without any lemon. Further, a light pudding, almost like gruel, would give me great pleasure." In a letter to his German music publisher, he begged wine—specifically the Rhine wine that always had been his favorite.

And he began to receive a congress of visitors as well. In Karl Holz's absence, Anton Schindler willingly had returned to do Beethoven's daily bidding, and during the succeeding weeks Schindler greeted and escorted to the composer's bedside current friends and benefactors, former friends now determined to set things straight, fellow musicians, his brother Johann, and a few strangers eager to meet the great man before it was too late. There came a daily visitor too, thirteen-year-old Gerhard von Breuning, the boy whom Beethoven nicknamed "Trouser Button" and whose company he delighted in. Breuning was drawn, in turn, to the grandfatherly demeanor of his family's longtime friend despite the fact that he clearly was dying. Austrian composers Antonio Diabelli, Jan Dolezálek, and Anselm Hüttenbrenner visited, some of them often. Composer Johann Hummel—who had been Beethoven's early friend and rival in Vienna—traveled to the *Schwarzspanierhaus* from as far away as his home in Weimar, bringing with him his wife and his fifteen-year-old pupil Ferdinand Hiller, introducing the boy whom Hummel insisted held great musical promise to the dying master in a manner that could not help but remind Beethoven of his own introduction to Mozart forty years before.

But although his spirits often were lifted high by the concern people expressed for him—and by the simple pleasures of their company—Beethoven's body continued to collapse. Two more abdominal tappings were required in February, and following the fourth, the long-suffering patient now recognized that his time was nearly done. "*Plaudite, amici, comoedia finita est*," he said with a hint of smile to Schindler and young Breuning on a day when Dr. Wawruch and his consultants had departed with grave expressions on their faces: "Applaud, friends, the comedy is finished."

At his brother's encouragement, Beethoven reluctantly agreed to receive the last rites of the church late in March, and on that same day the wine he had requested of his publisher arrived from Mainz. "Pity, pity—too late," he whispered to Schindler, who held a bottle for him to see, but then he spoke no more. He fell into a coma that evening, and didn't stir from it for two days, not until, in the midst of a late-afternoon snowstorm on March 26, with only Hüttenbrenner and an unknown woman—perhaps his maid, perhaps one of the two sisters-in-law he seldom had wanted to be near—at his bedside, a bright flash of lightning followed by a house-rattling clap of thunder roused him momentarily. He opened his eyes, raised his right hand and clenched it into a fist as if to spurn the sky's command, then his hand fell back to the bed. Ludwig van Beethoven was dead.

BECAUSE THE GREAT COMPOSER'S PASSING was an event of such moment in the city that had been his home for thirty-five years, artist Josef Danhauser had been permitted to come to Beethoven's bedroom to make a plaster death mask of his face and to execute drawings of his body in repose in a brightly polished coffin that stood near his bed—Beethoven's long hair falling away from his emaciated face and spreading across the pillow that held his head, his once-bright eyes now pressed closed, his body surrounded by flowers. But before they applied the plaster, reported Danhauser's brother Carl, who had accompanied him on the errand, the two men cut two locks of hair from the composer's temples as "souvenirs of the illustrious head."

In the decades before the invention of photography, it was more common than now for people to keep locks of hair as remembrances of children, parents, and lovers who had died, and to do the same when circumstances occasionally permitted with the hair of great and famous figures—such as the man whose long-battered body now lay on view. In the two days since Beethoven's death, Hüttenbrenner also had taken a keepsake lock of hair; Franz von Hartmann and his friend the young composer "Fritz" Schubert had cut two, and so did many others—friends, acquaintances, and strangers alike—

during the quiet hours before Beethoven's body was carried from his house.

In much the same way that they had been drawn for many decades to the pageantry and high emotion of operas and concerts, the people of Vienna also were renowned for their love of a fine and maudlin funeral, and an enormous crowd—20,000 people by some estimates—had surged into the Schwarzspanier-strasse by three o'clock on the afternoon of March 29, and as many of them as could manage it had pressed into the house's courtyard, where Beethoven's body now lay in state on an ornate bier. So many citizens of Vienna were eager to feel a part of the proceedings that it took ninety minutes for the funeral cortege to travel the four blocks to the Trinity Church of the Minorites in the Alsergasse. Eight *Kapellmeisters*, among them Johann Hummel, served as pallbearers; the city's leading musicians, many of whom had been Beethoven's close associates, carried torches; a choir made up of members of the Royal Court Opera sang the composer's own *Miserere*, adopted for voices for the occasion, and behind the coffin walked Gerhard von Breuning, his father, Stephan, Johann van Beethoven, the brother whom Beethoven had poorly attempted to love, and Johanna van Beethoven, the sister-in-law whom he vainly had tried to hate.

At the close of the requiem mass inside the church, the coffin was borne by a hearse hitched to four black horses, and it was followed by as many as two hundred horse-drawn coaches en route to the parish cemetery in the Währing district, where actor Heinrich Anschütz read a florid and worshipful oration composed for the occasion by beloved Vienna poet Franz Grillparzer. "We who stand here at the grave of the deceased

are in a sense the representatives of an entire nation . . ."
Anschütz intoned,

come to mourn the passing of one celebrated half of that
which remained to us from the vanished brilliance of the
art of our homeland . . . [Goethe,] the hero of poetry in
the German language and tongue still lives—and long
may he live. But the last master of resounding song, the
gracious mouth by which music spoke . . . has ceased to
be; and we stand weeping over the broken strings of an
instrument now stilled. . . .

Because he shut himself off from the world, they called
him hostile; and callous, because he shunned feelings.
[But] excess of feeling avoids feelings. He fled the world
because he did not find, in the whole compass of his loving nature, a weapon with which to resist it. He with-
drew from his fellowmen after he had given them everything and had received nothing in return. He remained
alone because he found no second self. But until his death
he preserved a human heart for all men, a father's heart
for his own people, the whole world. Thus he was, thus
he died, thus will he live for all time!

Return to your homes, then, distressed but composed.
And whenever, during your lives, the power of his works
overwhelms you like coming storm; when your rapture
pours out in the midst of a generation yet unborn, then
remember this hour and think: we were there when they
buried him, and when he died we wept!

The bright spring day had gone to dusk when Anschütz's words were finished and it was time to hammer Beethoven's coffin closed and lower it into the earth. He looked very different now, his visage altered utterly because death had claimed him, because of the changes the autopsy had wrought, but also because his head appeared as though it had been assailed by scissors—because so many adoring citizens had snipped keepsake locks of the great Beethoven's hair.

CODA

NEAR THE END OF HIS six-month sojourn in the village of
Heiligenstadt in the autumn of 1802, Ludwig van Beethoven
had become so distraught over his unrelenting deafness that for
a time he had considered summarily ending his life. But as he
explained to his brothers in the impassioned October letter he
chose never to mail, "only *my art* held me back. Ah, it seemed
impossible to leave the world until I had produced all that I felt
was within me, and so I spared this wretched life." By the time
his life did come to a close a quarter century later, he had created 138 singular and extraordinary compositions to which he
attached opus numbers, and two hundred more songs, canons,

and dances that he considered lesser works. In that time, the man who first and foremost considered himself a "tone poet" set classical music on a bold and impassioned and revolutionary new course, one from which it never would turn back, and he did so despite heartbreaking disappointments, crippling and defeating illnesses, and the deafness that ultimately robbed him of community as well as the aural pleasures of his music. His was a life shaped by tremendous passion and enduring pain, one shaped as well by his ability to draw from somewhere deep within him compositions that remain profoundly important to millions of people around the world two centuries after they were written. Out of this physically flawed and compromised man came music that by long-standing consensus has cast him as the artistic peer of Michelangelo Buonarroti, Leonardo da Vinci, and William Shakespeare, music that anchors him "at the center of human consciousness," in the view of British musicologist Burnett James. "Through the blending of the conscious and the unconscious in his extraordinarily deep and comprehensive experience of the farthest mysteries of this life," James wrote in the introduction to his book *Beethoven and Human Destiny*, "and above all in his overwhelming ability to embody in music the essence of that experience, Beethoven bears witness to the destiny of man."

Writing to his lifelong friend Franz Wegeler, Beethoven—who previously had confessed his hearing loss to Wegeler—nonetheless had been briefly buoyant about his prospects. He believed he was learning to cope with a world that was increasingly silent; he was newly in love with a woman who fascinated him, and he was sure that soon he would travel the world. "I will take fate by the throat, it shall not wholly over-come me," he had written. "Oh, it would be so lovely to live a thousand lives."

KARL BEETHOVEN, THE COMPOSER'S NEPHEW and sole heir, had died nine years before Ferdinand Hiller, in 1883, passed the small treasure he had clipped from the master com-poser's head to his only son. At seventy-one, Ferdinand Hiller's long career now was in its denouement; he still composed, much like the aging and infirm Beethoven had done, but—very unlike the man whom he briefly had met and thenceforth had hugely revered—already the public was losing interest in Hiller's creations, already his impact on the world of music was waning dramatically.

In the days before his death, Ludwig van Beethoven had urged fifteen-year-old Ferdinand Hiller to devote his life to art, and to work ceaselessly toward its perfection. Hiller had taken that admonition deeply to heart, and by all but the most demanding measurements, he had succeeded splendidly. While still a teenager, his talents had astonished some of Europe's foremost musicians; in Paris in his twenties, he had moved to the center of a circle of soon-to-be renowned young com-posers who were determined to infuse their music with tran-scendent emotion in the way that the now-deified Beethoven had done; and in the succeeding decades, Hiller had continued to be vitally important to both the legion of musicians whom he befriended and supported and the concertgoing public whose appreciation of music he nurtured at every turn. As his health deteriorated in the early 1880s and it became clear that his days too would soon be done, Ferdinand Hiller continued to compose, not because he hoped that posterity somehow would change its mind and one day demand his music, but simply because the joy of shaping sound into art remained synonymous with living for him.

BY THE TIME HE HAD given his long-cherished lock of Beethoven's hair to his son, Ferdinand Hiller had grown deeply distressed about the rise of rampant anti-Semitism in Europe, and he chillingly had predicted that because of it, the twentieth century would be filled with blood and horror. Paul Hiller and his family had begun to experience personally the effects of that ethnic hatred only a short time after his father's death, and although he, like his father, long had devoted his life to the best of Teutonic culture—to its musical arts—it was the Germany characterized by Hitler rather than by Beethoven in which he died unexpectedly in 1934, his wife and sons forced as they eulogized him to hide his Jewish heritage in the desperate hope of avoiding death themselves.

"Lust-murderers years are here," Marcel Hillaire, Paul Hiller's son born Erwin remembered his mother, Sophie, declaring to her two sons soon after her husband's death. "Cheat cleverly now, or run, or you will die." In Los Angeles late in his life, Marcel Hillaire wrote a lengthy manuscript—the unpublished book dedicated to Esther Taylor—in which he described his happy childhood in Cologne, the insidious rise of the Nazis, and his and his brother Edgar's separate decisions to leave Cologne when it became clear that "an immense Satanic reality had come to reign in our land." Edgar Hiller first had fled to Hamburg, where he had been employed by an opera company, and where he had presumed his Aryan-sounding surname would keep him safe from suspicion, yet after only a short time in the north he literally had been shouted from the stage in the midst of a performance because, a gaggle of operagoers bellowed, a Jew could not be permitted to perform the work of the great patriot Wagner. Following his expulsion from the stage, Edgar Hiller next had traveled uncertainly for a time—and perhaps went to Denmark, of course, although his brother's manuscript makes no mention of his several destinations—before he settled in Zurich in 1939, where he remained throughout the war, his promising singing career all but abandoned before it truly began.

For his part, Marcel—Erwin—already an actor, determined that the best place for him to hide was among his fellow performers in a traveling theater troupe. He dubbed himself Harry Fürster, and he performed itinerant roles ranging from Hamlet to country clowns, yet his huge attraction to feminine charms and his hearty carnal appetites continually got him into trouble, and occasionally very nearly cost him his life. It was his tryst with the troupe-manager's wife that led to his dismissal, as well as the manager's subsequent determination to reveal to German authorities the fact that young Herr Fürster was, in fact, a Jew. But another romance soon led—most improbably but propitiously—to his new lover's help in securing him a position as an office clerk in the "Organisation Todt," the Nazi army's construction corps. Posted to Brittany, where Todt workers were raising the line of defense known as the Atlantic Wall, and using his actual name again, Erwin Hiller rose far enough up the clerical ladder that eventually he answered directly to Todt chief Albert Speer. The position allowed him to stockpile surreptitiously an array of forged documents, one of which he employed to make it appear that the Third Reich was in desperate need in Brittany of the services of Frau Sophie Hiller. But as his mother was about to board a train in Cologne in the autumn of 1942 en route to join her son—the two of them hoping that she could find at least a modicum of security in France—Sophie Hiller was stricken by a heart attack and died.

Todt personnel and the whole of the German army in France had begun to retreat into Germany before Erwin Hiller's Jewish identity was discovered at last. He was jailed near Weimar and was condemned to death for his insidious deceit as much as his Semitic ancestry, but before his sentence could be carried out, he was transferred to a prison in Berlin, where, in the days before the war had commenced six years before, the mother of a teenaged girl who had adored Hiller had brought statutory rape charges against him. It was while he languished in Berlin, waiting to answer the accusation that he had had his way with an underaged girl, that the Russian army closed in on the city, liberating it and Erwin Hiller as well in April 1945.

It was not until three years later, however, that Erwin Hiller emigrated to the United States, and in June 1948 he now was Marcel Hillaire as he walked the streets of New York, the nominally "French" actor assuming that prospects in America would not be bright for a German, regardless of his ethnicity. Marcel remained in New York for six years, working for a time as a lowly busboy, but eventually securing a series of character roles in theater and on television. Edgar Hiller, who had spent the preceding decade in Zurich, briefly had joined his brother in the beginning, but somehow America simply was too foreign for him—its musical milieu impossible to break into, it appeared—and so he returned to Hamburg, the city where he had been booed off a stage a decade before, and where he would live until his death on November 20, 1959, his demise at only age fifty-three caused by a chronic and deep depression and his determination simply to stop eating.

Marcel Hillaire had lived in Los Angeles for five years when he learned of his brother's death, one that he guiltily believed he might have prevented—had he insisted that Edgar remain in the United States with him, had he at least remained in more constant touch and somehow done more to keep his brother's spirits bright. Yet beginning in the mid-1950s, Marcel Hillaire, the debonair "Frenchman," at last had begun to be in great demand. He won supporting roles in the film *Sabrina* in 1954 and in episodes of television's *Twilight Zone* in 1959; and in the 1960s, he emerged as Hollywood's consummate continental character actor, appearing in dozens of films, among them *Seven Thieves, The Four Horsemen of the Apocalypse, Take Her, She's Mine, Murderers' Row,* and Woody

Allen's *Take the Money and Run*, as well as numerous television series that included *Adventures in Paradise, The Man from
U.N.C.L.E., I Spy,* and *Mission Impossible*.

He worked far less in the years that followed his nearly fatal
injury in the spring of 1974—the eight years he spent in the
constant company of Esther Taylor—a time during which he
played host with easy but enthusiastic aplomb to a living room
concert several evenings a week, each program carefully culled
from his operatic and orchestral record collection, the audience often solely the two of them and their menagerie of cats
and birds. Marcel's favorite composers were the Romantics—
and Romanticism boldly began with Beethoven, he would in-
sist to his "Estherchen" before reminding her as well that he
might have possessed to that very day a lock of the great
Beethoven's hair had not his dear but surely misguided father
chosen to give it to the collective populace of the whole of the
Rhineland instead.

Marcel Hillaire developed bladder cancer in 1987 and chose
to undergo experimental surgery at the close of that year.
While still hospitalized two weeks following his operation, a
sudden pulmonary embolism ended his life on January 1,
1988. Because their friend for so long had vehemently opposed
religion of every kind—haunted as he was by the horrors he
personally had witnessed being carried out in religion's
name—Esther Taylor, now a wife and the mother of a young
son, and Marcel's longtime friend, the actor Richard Angarola,
chose to honor his life simply by gathering together the people who deeply cared about him, briefly remembering the joy

he had brought to them, then scattering his ashes into the nearby Pacific.

WE LIKELY WILL NEVER KNOW whether Edgar Hiller did, in fact, travel to Denmark in the days and months that followed his musical expulsion from Hamburg, and neither will we ever be sure of the path taken by the lock of hair between Cologne and little Gilleleje. What is certain, however, is that as the twentieth century came to a close in the small seaport positioned alongside the place where the narrow Øresund meets the open waters of the Kattegat Sea, the events that occurred in the autumn of 1943 were seldom openly discussed, yet they were far from forgotten. Inside a recently constructed building that housed the community's library as well as its museum, a second-story wing flush with photographs, artifacts, and maps memorialized the remarkable success of Gilleleje's citizens in saving thirteen hundred Jews from capture by the Nazis. On the lawn outside—from which vantage point visitors could view the dark and often-unsettled sea as well as the distant coastal hills of Sweden—stood a statue of a stylized bronze figure, one hand raised in jubilation, the other holding a ram's horn whose sound surely is that of freedom. Crafted by Israeli sculptor George Weil and titled "The Great Blast of the Shofar," the horn's sound signifying the survival of the Jewish people, the statue had been a gift from the Israeli government in 1997, a moving acknowledgment that there were indeed pockets of heroism and profound humanity in the midst of the horrors of the Holocaust, and that perhaps one of the foremost was the Danish town of Gilleleje.

On its surface, Gilleleje seemed little changed from the way it must have appeared in October 1943, but almost all of those who were active in the rescue effort now were dead. Julius Jørgensen, the retired fisherman whose father was caretaker of the church during the rescue days, was a widower and had grown infirm, but his eyes remained bright as he smoked his trademark tiny cigars and remembered a distant time that continued to make him proud. A physician, Dr. Steffen Herman, now lived and worked by chance in the same house and clinic that Kay and Marta Fremming had built; the small harbor continued to protect a fleet of fishing schooners, and the loft of the Gilleleje Church still looked almost exactly as it had on the morning after screaming Gestapo agents had forced ten dozen refugees to descend from it more than fifty years before.

Michele Wassard Larsen, once a girl in Gilleleje, turned sixty in January 1999 and retired from the library job she had held for many years. Although the Danish island of Sjælland had been her home for more than half a century, she still longed for her native country, and talked openly and often with her son Thomas about the possibility that she would choose to live out her retirement years near her sister Rolande in a quiet village in the south of France. Michele's adoptive mother, Marta Fremming, ninety years old and entirely unaware of her surroundings, died in her sleep on June 6, 1999. Michele suspected that even if she had been able to quiz her mother at length before her memory had been stolen by disease about how her father had come to possess a much-traveled lock of Beethoven's hair, she would have learned nothing more. If Marta had harbored secrets about the hair, Michele believed she surely would have shared them with her on the day when she first had shown her the locket, and Michele now strongly suspected that Kay Fremming had kept the details of the giving hidden from even his wife.

"When I look back and think that apparently we were not meant to find the secret of the locket, I can't help but wonder why," Michele wrote as the new century dawned, but her son Thomas believed there was an answer to that query that made sense to him, at least. "Keeping the locket on the wall in my living room one day would have made me proud, but it never could have given me an experience similar to those I have had in the years since it was sold. I never would have truly learned about Beethoven, his music and his life. And I never would have met and communicated with so many people around the world once we began to search for the secret."

Although the search by now had slowed dramatically—new leads surfacing only occasionally—it nonetheless had moved into its second century. Michele Wassard Larsen and her son continued to pursue each hopeful possibility that presented itself, and they seldom were discouraged by yet another dead end because they understood that the deepest mysteries were, of course, the most compelling kind.

THE LOCK OF HAIR THAT Ira Brilliant and Che Guevara purchased from Michele Wassard Larsen had achieved real notoriety in the years since it had traveled to America, and it wasn't surprising therefore that its monetary value had increased dramatically as well. Although none of the 582 strands of hair from the great composer's head were for sale—or probably ever would be—it was illustrative of their crescendoing worth when, in the summer of 1998, a Beethoven enthusiast in Michigan paid $3,700 for *two* strands of purported Beethoven hair that had been wrongly, if not fraudulently, guaranteed by R&R Enterprises of Bedford, New Hampshire, as having been culled from the now renowned Guevara lock. When Ira Brilliant cried foul after being contacted by the suspicious buyer, the Michigan man at last succeeded in getting his money returned, and the auction house in the end apologized profusely for what it claimed was its unfortunate "textual error."

The bona fide relic, on the other hand—the one currently in safe repose in San Jose as well as its companion strands in Nogales—had been responsible during the preceding five years for setting in motion an unlikely but inspiriting adventure. Brilliant remained quick to admit that had it not been for the sudden enthusiasm of Che Guevara as well as the insistence of Beethoven Center director William Meredith, curator Patricia Stroh, and board president Tom Wendel, he might never have pursued the lock of hair, and therefore might never have had the profound experience of holding it in his hands. At the time of the Sotheby's auction, Brilliant's attention had been fixed on the Opus 1 first edition—*that* was the treasure he longed to obtain for the center. Yet beginning with the days during which the storied locket with a coil of hair inside had sat unopened on his desk, and in the months and years that had followed, its singular trip through time, the still-mysterious role it played in the salvation of one or perhaps many Jewish refugees, and the arresting explanation it lately had offered about the composer's medical torments all combined to make him enormously grateful that his friends had pressed him into action in December 1994, and that he alone had begun to pursue his uncommon passion twenty years before. "My original hopes for a meaningful life have been reified," he wrote just days before the century turned, nine months prior to his seventy-eighth birthday, "and I'll carry with me forever the satisfaction of knowing that I am responsible for bringing so many people into this grand adventure."

And there had been one more satisfaction for Ira Brilliant along the way: with the help of antiquarian music dealer Albi Rosenthal in London, he had been able at last to purchase a fine first edition of the Opus 1 Piano Trios, which he had presented to the Beethoven Center that bore his name at a gala celebration in October 1997, the occasion marking his and his wife Irma's fiftieth wedding anniversary, by now fully half of their years together shared rather intimately with Ludwig van Beethoven as well.

For Che Guevara, being the steward of a lock of hair for these five years had connected him to the composer and his music even more profoundly and intimately than he had been before that time. For three decades, Beethoven had taught him an enormous amount about suffering, yet the composer also had demonstrated to him at least as much about the way in which suffering could be overcome, and the physician remained astounded to think that something of the master remained very literally alongside him each day as he did his work.

In the first days of the new century, Che Guevara and neuroscientist William Walsh had begun work on the paper they hoped to complete in time to present at one of the several scientific conferences that would welcome it that autumn, and Beethoven Center director William Meredith increasingly was busy planning the "Beethoven Treasures in America" exhibition that was slated to open at the Library of Congress in Washington, D.C., in April 2001, where the Guevara lock of the composer's hair would be displayed outside San Jose for the first time. Meredith, the Beethoven Center's only permanent director since its inception in 1983, long ago had turned his passion for Beethoven's music into his academic concentration and subsequently into the locus of his career, and he could not help but be astounded by the miraculous possibility that what had begun as a simple sentimental act—Ferdinand Hiller's innocent snipping of a bit of hair from the head of that man of genius—had, in the end, resulted in the resolution of some of the fundamental questions about Ludwig van Beethoven's life.

IN THE SUN-SOAKED JULY OF 2000, Bill Meredith and members of the American Beethoven Society hosted a gathering in San Jose to which were invited the people who had played key roles in the selling and subsequent buying of

Beethoven's hair back in 1994, everyone who had struggled—
so far still in vain—to determine precisely how the hair had
fled from Germany and ultimately had been made a gift in
Gilleleje, as well as those people who successfully had unrav-
eled the hair's forensic secrets. Michele Wassard Larsen and her
son Thomas flew from Denmark for the simple but nonetheless august occasion; Ira Brilliant and Che Guevara attended, to
be sure; so did Bill Walsh, the forensic project's chief scientist;
so too Esther Taylor, Marcel Hillaire's friend and heir, the sole
living tie to Ferdinand Hiller's family.

The far-flung group met simply to connect faces with names
at long last, to celebrate the huge improbabilities and little mir-
acles that at least briefly had linked their lives, and collectively,
of course, they viewed once more the bit of brown and gray
hair that they continued to cherish in their separate yet
nonetheless similar ways. Like the bones of ancient Christian
martyrs that were considered to be sacramental, like the venerated bodies of deceased Tibetan Buddhist Dalai Lamas, the
long-treasured lock of Beethoven's hair was a true relic—a
physical remnant of a once-living human being that kept the
spirit of that person present and somehow wonderfully alive.
And in Ludwig van Beethoven's case, how fitting it seemed
that it was his *hair* that had survived. The wild mane that had
framed his dark face in his waning years had characterized his
unruly temperament as much as his arresting personal presence; it was symbolic of his enduring eccentricity as well as his
certain genius; it echoed his artistry; it pointed indeed to his
pain; and when Ferdinand Hiller and so many others clipped

his hair as keepsakes in the last days of March 1827, they did so because they believed his music long since had proven that it would survive through the ages.

In each succeeding era that has followed his death, Beethoven's music has seemed fresh and vital and reflective of something essential about the human experience. "Perhaps that shared experience is suffering," Bill Meredith observed, "perhaps it is hope, but whatever it is, somehow Beethoven captured in his music something impossible to codify that has transformed people for nearly two centuries."

It was his music's ability literally to change the lives of the people who heard it that had led Ferdinand Hiller to clip the lock, then treasure it throughout his life, that had made it a profound kind of gift in a time of terrible crisis, that had brought it to America with the most eager anticipation, that had stirred the examination of its chemical secrets. And it was the transforming might of Beethoven's music as well that drew an otherwise entirely disparate group to California that summer to honor the relic together.

By the time of the summer gathering, Brilliant, Guevara, and Meredith had succeeded in locating the Beethoven skull fragments that had been studied in Vienna in the 1980s, and their current owner had allowed testing of the bone to begin, both to verify the dramatic lead finding and, via DNA comparison, to attempt to prove that both hair and bone had come from the same person.

A DNA match would be extraordinary, particularly for this reason: for the first time in the 170 years since Ferdinand Hiller had insisted to his comrade composers in Paris that the lock of hair they delighted in had come from the master's head; in the eighty-eight years since Paul Hiller had hoped a Cologne frame maker could renew the locket in which the hair was harbored; in the fifty-six years since Kay Fremming had nodded in assent as the hair was pressed into his huge hands; since Che Guevara first had exposed the hair to forensic inquiry four years before, finally it would be certain beyond any doubt that the treasured lock that had made that improbable journey and along the way had transformed so many lives, was, quite wonderfully, *Beethoven's* hair.

ACKNOWLEDGMENTS

THIS BOOK HAD ITS BEGINNING when my agent, Jody Rein, believed it could be one, and I thank her for her instincts, her insight, and her heart. John Sterling and William Shinker championed it early on, and I am grateful; Luke Dempsey was a splendid editor and always a calming and encouraging friend, and many people at Broadway Books lent the book their exemplary talents as it wended its way into print. A hundred thanks to them all.

It would have been impossible to gather together the myriad stories presented here without the invaluable assistance of many far-flung people. In Denmark, dozens were helpful,

among them most particularly Anne Sørensen, Christian Tortzen, Paul Sandfort, Julius Jørgensen, Sanne Bloch, Therkel Stræde, Christian Pedersen, Tereza Burmeister, Anne Lehmann, Ulf Haxen, and Rasmus Kreth.

In Germany, Hans-Werner Küthen at the Beethoven-Archiv in Bonn offered early support, and researcher Alexander Fülling in Gummersbach made critical discoveries virtually every time one was sorely needed. Christian Jesserer and Manfred Skopec in Vienna, Myriam Provence in Paris, Robert Eagle in London, and Oxana Korol and Richard Oestermann in Jerusalem offered vital help. In the United States, Patricia Stroh, Robert Portillo, Leo Goldberger, Stan Lindaas, Richard Angarola, Werner Baumgartner, Marcia Eisenberg, Amy Foxson, Erwin Hiller (no relation), Kathleen Jacobs, and Maury Calder each offered specific and very critical assistance. Karen Holmgren, Dottie Peacock, and Ruth Slickman gave me wonderful reassurances along the way, which I could not have done without.

I am enormously indebted as well to the people about whom I wrote who so generously shared their time and memories with me. Michele Wassard Larsen and Thomas Wassard Larsen were extraordinarily willing to help uncover the secrets of the lock of hair that once was theirs, and along the way they have been more kind than I can describe. Bill Meredith, the director of the Beethoven Center in San Jose, offered vital criticism and warm support every step of the way. Esther Taylor, the sole living link to the Hiller family, responded to a very unusual telephone call with immediate interest and enthusiasm and a treasure trove of information. Bill Walsh, scientist and

ACKNOWLEDGMENTS

humanitarian, patiently explained complex material and worked diligently to produce unassailable test results. Dr. Alfredo "Che" Guevara shared his infectious enthusiasm and his particular passion and made me feel in every way like a *compadre*. And nearly every day for more than two years, Ira Brilliant was eager to answer questions, point me in the proper direction, and ceaselessly affirm that the music of Beethoven matters enormously. A thousand thanks to each of them.

To readers who desire to learn more about the life and legacy of the composer, I recommend membership in the American Beethoven Society (San Jose State University, One Washington Square, San Jose, California, 95192–0171, telephone 408–924–4590), which includes a subscription to the authoritative *Beethoven Journal*, published semiannually.